THE BROCKHAMPTON LIBRARY

book of
Boys' Names

BROCKHAMPTON PRESS
LONDON

Aaron mountaineer, enlightener (*Hebrew*); a contracted diminutive is **Arn**.

Abe father (*Aramaic*); diminutive of **Abraham, Abram**.

Abel breath, fickleness, vanity (*Hebrew*).

Abraham father of a multitude (*Hebrew*); diminutive forms are **Abe, Bram**.

Abram father of elevation (*Hebrew*); diminutive forms are **Abe, Bram**.

Adair a Scottish form of **Edgar**.

Adam man, earth man, red earth (*Hebrew*).

Adin sensual (*Hebrew*).

Adler eagle, perceptive one (*Germanic*).

Adney island-dweller (*Old English*).

Adrian of the Adriatic in Italy (*Latin*); a variant form is **Hadrian**.

Adriel from God's congregation (*Hebrew*).

Ahern horse lord, horse owner (*Irish Gaelic*).

Aidan fire, flame (*Irish Gaelic*); a variant form is **Edan**.

Ainsley a surname, meaning meadow of the respected one, used as a first name (*Old English*).

Ainslie a Scottish form of **Ainsley**, used as a first name.

Al diminutive of **Alan, Albert**, and names beginning Al-.

Alan meaning uncertain, possibly a hound (*Slavonic*), harmony (*Celtic*); variant forms are **Allan, Allen**.

Alard a variant form of **Allard**.

Alasdair, Alastair variant forms of **Alister**.

Albern noble warrior (*Old English*).

Albert all-bright; illustrious (*Germanic*); diminutive forms are **Al, Bert, Bertie**.

Alden a surname, meaning old or trustworthy friend, used as a first name (*Old English*).

Alder a surname, meaning alder tree, used as a first name (*Old English*).

Aldis a surname, meaning old house, used as a first name (*Old English*).

Aldo, Aldous old (*Germanic*).

Aldrich a surname, meaning old, wise ruler, used as a first name (*Old English*).

Alec, Aleck diminutive forms of **Alexander**.

Aled the name of a river used as a first name (*Welsh*).

Alex diminutive of **Alexander**; a variant form is **Alix**.

Alexander a helper of men (*Greek*); diminutive forms are **Alec, Alex, Alick, Lex, Sandy**.

Alexis help; defence (*Greek*).

Alf, Alfie diminutive forms of **Alfred**.

Alfred good or wise counsellor (*Germanic*); diminutive forms are **Alf, Alfie**.

Alger elf spear (*Old English*).

Algernon whiskered (*Old French*); a diminutive form is **Algie, Algy**.

Alick diminutive of **Alexander**, now used independently.

Alister the Scots Gaelic form of **Alexander**; variant forms are **Alasdair, Alastair**.

Allan, Allen variant forms of **Alan**.

Allard noble and brave (*Old English*); a variant form is **Alard**.

Aloysius a Latin form of **Lewis**.

Alpha first one (*Greek*).

Alpheus exchange (*Hebrew*).

Alpin blond (*Scottish Gaelic*).

Alroy red-haired (*Scottish Gaelic*).

Altman old, wise man (*Germanic*).

Alton a surname, meaning old stream or source, used as a first name (*Old English*).

Alun the Welsh form of **Alan**.

Alvah exalted one (*Hebrew*).

Alvin, Alwin winning all (*Old English*).

Amadeus lover of God (*Latin*).

Ambrose immortal (Greek).

Amery a variant form of **Amory**.

Ammon hidden (*Egyptian*).

Amory famous ruler (*Germanic*); variant forms are **Amery, Emery, Emmery**.

Amos bearer of a burden (*Hebrew*).

Anatole from the East (*Greek*).

Andie diminutive of **Andrew**.

André the French form of **Andrew**, becoming popular as an English-language form.

Andreas Greek, Latin, and German forms of **Andrew**.

Andrew strong; manly; courageous (*Greek*); diminutive forms are **Andie, Andy, Dandie, Drew**.

Aneirin, Aneurin noble, modest (*Welsh*); a diminutive form is **Nye**.

Angus excellent virtue (*Gaelic*); a diminutive form is **Gus**.

Anselm, Ansel a surname, meaning, god helmet, i.e. under the protection of God, used as a first name (*Germanic*).

Ansley a surname, meaning clearing with a hermitage or solitary dwelling, used as a first name (*Old English*).

Anthony a variant form of **Antony**; a diminutive form is **Tony**.

Antoine the French form of **Anthony**, now used independently as an English-language form; a variant form is **Antwan**.

Anton a German form of **Antony**, now used as an English-language form.

Antony priceless; praiseworthy (*Latin*); a variant form is **Anthony**; a diminutive form is **Tony**.

Antwan a variant form of **Antoine**.

Anwell beloved (*Gaelic*).

Anyon anvil (*Gaelic*).

Aonghas Scots Gaelic form of **Angus**.

Archard sacred and powerful (*Germanic*).

Archibald very bold; holy prince (*Germanic*); diminutive forms are **Archie, Archy**.

Ardal high valour (*Irish Gaelic*).

Ardley from the domestic meadow (*Old English*).

Argus all-seeing, watchful one, from Argus Panoptes, a character from Greek mythology with a hundred eyes all over his body (*Greek*).

Aric sacred ruler (*Old English*); diminutive forms are **Rick, Rickie, Ricky**.

Ariel God's lion (*Hebrew*).

Arlen pledge (*Irish Gaelic*).

Arlie, Arley, Arly a surname, meaning eagle wood, used as a first name (*Old English*).

Armel stone prince or chief (*Breton Gaelic*).

Armstrong a surname, meaning strong in the arm, used as a first name (*Old English*).

Arn diminutive of **Arnold**, a contraction of **Aaron**.

Arnall a surname variant form of **Arnold** used as a first name (*Germanic*).

Arnatt, Arnett surname variant forms of **Arnold** used as first names.

Arno a diminutive of **Arnold**.

Arnold strong as an eagle (*Germanic*); eagle meadow (*Old English*); diminutive forms are **Arn, Arnie, Arno, Arny**.

Arnott a surname variant form of **Arnold** used as a first name.

Arthur eagle Thor (*Celtic*); a diminutive form is **Art**.

Arval, Arvel greatly lamented (*Latin*).

Arvid eagle wood (*Norse*).

Arvin people's friend (*Germanic*).

Arwel meaning uncertain (*Welsh*).

Arwyn muse (*Welsh*); a variant form is **Awen**.

Asa healer, physician (*Hebrew*).

Asahel made of God (*Hebrew*).

Asaph a collector (*Hebrew*).

Ashley, Ashleigh the surname, meaning ash wood or glade, used as a first name (*Old English*).

Ashlin ash-surrounded pool (*Old English*).

Ashton an English placename, meaning ash-tree farmstead, used as a first name (*Old English*).

Ashur martial, warlike (*Semitic*).

Athol, Atholl a placename and surname, meaning new Ireland, used as a first name (*Scots Gaelic*).

Atlee, Atley, Atley a surname, meaning at the wood or clearing, used as a first name (*Old English*).

Auberon noble bear (*Germanic*); a variant form is **Oberon**; a diminutive form is **Bron**.

Aubin a surname, meaning blond one, used as a first name (*French*).

Aubrey ruler of spirits (*Germanic*).

August the Polish and German form of **Augustus**; the eighth month of the year, named after the Roman emperor **Augustus**, used as a first name.

Augustine belonging to **Augustus** (*Latin*); a diminutive form is **Gus**.

Augustus exalted; imperial (*Latin*); a diminutive form is **Gus**.

Aurelius golden (*Latin*).

Austin a contraction of **Augustine**.

Awen a variant form of **Arwyn**.

Axton stone of the sword fighter (*Old English*).

Bailey, Baillie a surname, meaning bailiff or steward, used as a first name (*Old French*); a variant form is **Bayley**.

Baird a Scottish surname, meaning minstrel or bard, used as a first name (*Celtic*); a variant form is **Bard**.

Balfour a surname from a Scottish placename, meaning village with pasture, used as a first name (*Scots Gaelic*).

Ballard a surname, meaning bald, used as a first name (*Old English/ Old French*).

Baptist a baptiser, purifier (*Greek*).

Baptiste a French form of **Baptist**.

Barclay a surname, meaning birch wood, used as a first name (*Old English*); variant forms are **Berkeley, Berkley**.

Bard a variant form of **Baird**; a diminutive form of **Bardolph**.

Bardolph bright wolf (*Germanic*).

Barlow a surname, meaning barley hill or clearing, used as a first name (*Old English*).

Barnaby, Barnabas son of consolation and exhortation (*Hebrew*); a diminutive form is **Barney**.

Barnard a variant form of **Bernard**; a diminutive form is **Barney**.

Barnet, Barnett a surname, meaning land cleared by burning, used as a first name (*Old English*).

Baron the lowest rank of the peerage used as a first name (*Old French*); a variant form is **Barron**.

Barratt, Barrett a surname, meaning commerce or strife, used as a first name (*Old French*).

Barron a variant form of **Baron**.

Barry spear (*Irish Gaelic*).

Bart a diminutive form of **Bartholomew, Bartley, Barton, Bartram**.

Barthold variant form of **Berthold**.

Bartholomew a warlike son (*Hebrew*); a diminutive forms is **Bart**.

Barton a surname, meaning farm or farmyard, used as a first name (*Old English*); a diminutive form is **Bart**.

Bartram a variant form of **Bertram**.

Basil kingly, royal (*Greek*).

Baxter a surname, meaning baker, used as a first name (*Old English*).

Bayley a variant form of **Bailey**.

Beau handsome (*French*); a diminutive form of **Beaufort**, **Beamont**.

Beaufort a surname, meaning beautiful stronghold, used as a first name (*French*); a diminutive form is **Beau**.

Beaumont a surname, meaning beautiful hill, used as a first name (*French*); a diminutive form is **Beau**.

Beavan, Beaven variant forms of **Bevan**.

Bellamy a surname, meaning handsome friend, used as a first name (*Old French*).

Ben a diminutive form of **Benedict, Benjamin**, also used independently.

Benedict, Benedick blessed (*Latin*); *also* **Bennet**; diminutives are **Ben, Bennie, Benny**.

Benjamin son of the right hand (*Hebrew*); diminutive forms are **Ben, Benjie, Bennie, Benny**.

Benjie a diminutive form of **Benjamin**.

Bennet a variant form of **Benedict**.

Bennie, Benny a diminutive form of **Benedict, Benjamin**.

Benson a surname, meaning son of **Ben**, now used as a first name.

Bentley a surname from a Yorkshire placename, meaning woodland clearing where bent-grass grows, used as a first name (*Old English*).

Berkeley, Berkley variant forms of **Barclay**.

Bernard strong or hardy bear (*Germanic*); *also* **Barnard**; diminutive forms are **Barney, Bernie**.

Bernhard, Bernhardt a German form of **Bernard**.

Bernie a diminutive form of **Bernard**.

Bert the diminutive form of **Albert, Bertram, Egbert, Gilbert**, etc.

Berthold bright ruler (*Ger-*

manic); variant forms are **Barthold, Bertold, Berthoud**; diminutive forms are **Bert, Bertie**.

Bertie diminutive forms of **Albert, Bertram, Egbert, Gilbert, Herbert**, etc.

Bertold, Berthoud variant forms of **Berthold**.

Bertram bright; fair; illustrious (*Germanic*); a variant form is **Bartram**; diminutive forms are **Bert, Bertie**.

Bertrand the French form of **Bertram**.

Bevan a surname, meaning son of **Evan**, used as a first name (*Welsh*); variant forms are **Beavan, Beaven, Bevin**.

Beverley, Beverly a placename, meaning beaver stream, used as a first name (*Old English*); a diminutive form is **Bev**; also used as a girl's name.

Bevin a surname, meaning drink wine, used as a first name; a variant form of Bevan.

Bevis bull (*French*).

Bill, Billie diminutive forms of **William**.

Bing a surname, meaning a hollow, used as a first name (*Germanic*).

Blair a placename and surname,

meaning a plain, used as a first name (*Scottish Gaelic*).

Blaise sprouting forth (*French*).

Blake pale or fair-complexioned (*Old English*).

Bleddyn wolf (*Welsh*).

Blyth, Blythe a surname, meaning cheerful and gentle, used as a first name (*Old English*).

Bob, Bobbie, Bobby diminutive forms of **Robert**.

Bonar a surname, meaning gentle, kind, courteous, used as a first name (*French*); variant forms are **Bonnar, Bonner**.

Bonnar, Bonner variant forms of **Bonar**.

Booth a surname, meaning hut or shed, used as a first name (*Old Norse*).

Boris small (*Russian*).

Bowie a surname, meaning yellow-haired, used as a first name (*Scots Gaelic*).

Boyce a surname, meaning a wood, used as a first name (*Old French*).

Boyd a surname, meaning light-haired, used as a first name (*Scots Gaelic*).

Boyne the name of an Irish river, meaning white cow, used as a first name (*Irish Gaelic*).

Brad a diminutive form of

Bradley, now used independently.

Bradley a surname, meaning broad clearing or wood, used as a first name (*Old English*); a diminutive form is **Brad**.

Brady a surname, of unknown meaning, used as a first name (*Irish Gaelic*).

Bram a diminutive form of **Abram, Abraham**.

Bramwell a surname, meaning from the bramble spring, sometimes used as a first name (*Old English*).

Brandon a surname, meaning broom-covered hill, used as a first name (*Old English*); a variant form of **Brendan**.

Brendan prince (*Celtic*); a variant form is **Brandon**.

Brent a surname, meaning a steep place, used as a first name (*Old English*).

Bret, Brett a Breton (*Old French*).

Brewster a surname, meaning brewer, used as a first name (*Old English*).

Brian strong (*Celtic*); a variant form is **Bryan**.

Brice a surname, of unknown meanng, used as a first name (*Celtic*); a variant form is **Bryce**.

Broderic, Broderick a surname, meaning son of Roderick, used as a first name (*Welsh*); brother (*Scots Gaelic*).

Brodie, Brody a surname, meaning ditch, used as a first name (*Scots Gaelic*).

Bron a diminutive form of **Auberon, Oberon**.

Brook, Brooke a surname, meaning stream, used as a first name.

Bruce a surname, meaning unknown, used as a first name (*Old French*).

Bruno brown (*Germanic*).

Bryan a variant form of **Brian**.

Bryce a variant form of **Brice**.

Bryn hill (*Welsh*).

Buck stag; he-goat; a lively young man (*Old English*).

Budd, Buddy the informal term for a friend or brother used as a first name (*American English*).

Burgess a surname, meaning citizen or inhabitant of a borough, used as a first name (*Old French*).

Burley dweller in the castle by the meadow (*Old English*); a diminutive form is **Burleigh**.

Burnett a surname, meaning brown-complexioned or brown-haired, used as a first name (*Old French*).

Burt a diminutive form of **Burton**, now used independently.

Burton a surname, meaning farmstead of a fortified placed, used as a first name (*Old English*); a diminutive form is **Burt**.

Buster an informal term of address for a boy or young man, now used as a first name (*American English*).

Byrne a variant form of **Burn**.

Byron a surname, meaning at the cowsheds, used as a first name (*Old English*).

Cadell a surname, meaning battle spirit, used as a first name (*Welsh*).

Cadmus man from the east; in mythology a Phoenician prince who founded Thebes with five warriors he had created (*Greek*).

Caesar long-haired; the Roman title of emperor used as a first name (*Latin*).

Cain possession; the Biblical character who killed his brother Abel (*Hebrew*).

Calder a placename and surname, meaning hard or rapid water, used as a first name (*Celtic*).

Caleb a dog (*Hebrew*); a diminutive form is **Cale**.

Caley thin, slender (*Irish Gaelic*); diminutive form of **Calum**.

Calhoun a surname, meaning from the forest, used as a first name (*Irish Gaelic*).

Callisto most fair or good (*Greek*).

Calum, Callum the Scots Gaelic form of *Columba*, the Latin for dove; a diminutive form of **Malcolm**; diminutive forms are **Cally, Caley**.

Calvert a surname, meaning calf herd, used as a first name (*Old English*).

Calvin little bald one (*Latin*).

Cameron a surname, meaning hook nose, used as a first name (*Scots Gaelic*).

Campbell a surname, meaning crooked mouth, used as a first name (*Scots Gaelic*).

Canice handsome or fair one (*Irish Gaelic*).

Caradoc, Caradog beloved (*Welsh*); a variant form is **Cradoc**.

Cardew a surname meaning black fort, used as a first name (*Welsh*).

Carey a surname, meaning castle dweller (*Welsh*) or son of the dark one (*Irish Gaelic*), used as a first name; a variant form of **Cary**.

Carl an anglicized German and Swedish form of **Charles**; a diminutive form of **Carlton, Carleton**.

Carleton a variant form of **Carlton**.

Carlton a placename and surname, meaning farm of the churls—a rank of peasant, now used as a first name (*Old English*); variant forms are **Carleton, Charlton, Charleton**; a diminutive form is **Carl**.

Carmichael a Scottish placename and surname, meaning fort of **Michael**, used as a first name (*Celtic*).

Carol a shortened form of *Carolus*, the Latin form of **Charles**; also used as a girl's name.

Carr a placename and surname, meaning overgrown marshy ground, used as a first name (*Old Norse*); variant forms are **Karr, Kerr**.

Carrick a placename, meaning rock, used as a first name (*Gaelic*).

Carson a surname, of uncertain meaning but possibly marsh dweller (*Old English*), used as a first name.

Carter a surname, meaning a driver or maker of carts (*Old English*), or son of Arthur (*Scots Gaelic*), used as a first name.

Carwyn blessed love (*Welsh*).

Cary a surname, meaning pleasant stream, used as a first name (*Celtic*); a variant form is **Carey**.

Casey an Irish surname, meaning vigilant, used as a first name; a placename, Cayce in Kentucky, where the hero Casey Jones was born, used as a first name (*Irish Gaelic*).

Cashel a placename, meaning circular stone fort, used as a first name (*Irish Gaelic*).

Caspar, Casper the Dutch form of **Jasper**, now also used as an English-language form.

Cassian, Cassius a Roman family name, of uncertain meaning—possibly empty, used as a first name (*Latin*); a diminutive form is **Cass**.

Cassidy a surname, meaning clever, used as a first name (*Irish Gaelic*); a diminutive form is **Cass**.

Castor beaver (*Greek*).

Cathal battle ruler (*Irish Gaelic*).

Cato a Roman family name, meaning wise one, used as a first name (*Latin*).

Cavan a placename, meaning hollow with a grassy hill, used as a first name (*Irish Gaelic*); a variant form is **Kavan**.

Cecil dim-sighted (*Latin*).

Cedric a name adapted by Sir Walter Scott for a character in *Ivanhoe* from the Saxon *Cerdic*, the first king of Wessex.

Ceinwen beautiful and blessed (*Welsh*).

Chad meaning uncertain—possibly warlike, bellicose (*Old English*).

Chancellor a surname, meaning counsellor or secretary, used as a first name (*Old French*).

Chancey a variant form of **Chauncey**.

Chandler a surname, meaning maker or seller of candles, used as a first name (*Old French*).

Chapman a surname, meaning merchant, used as a first name (*Old English*).

Charles strong; manly; noble-spirited (*Germanic*); a diminutive form is **Charlie**.

Charlton, Charleton variant forms of **Carlton**.

Chase a surname, meaning hunter, used as a first name (*Old French*).

Chauncey, Chaunce a surname, of uncertain meaning—possibly chancellor, used as a first name (Old French); variant forms are **Chance, Chancey**.

Chester a placename, meaning Roman fortified camp, used as a first name (*Old English*).

Chris a diminutive form of **Christian, Christopher**.

Christian belonging to Christ; a believer in Christ (*Latin*); diminutive forms are **Chris, Christie, Christy**.

Christie a surname, meaning Christian, used as a first name; a diminutive form of **Christian, Christopher** a diminutive

form of **Christian**; a variant
form is **Christy**.

Christopher bearing Christ
(*Greek*); diminutive forms are
**Chris, Christie, Christy,
Kester, Kit**.

Christy a variant form of
Christie.

Cian ancient (*Irish Gaelic*);
anglicized forms are **Kean,
Keane**.

Ciarán small and black (*Irish
Gaelic*); the anglicized form is
Kieran.

Claiborne a variant form of
Clayborne; a diminutive form
is **Clay**.

Clarence bright, shining (*Latin*);
a diminutive form is **Clarrie**.

Clark, Clarke a surname,
meaning cleric, scholar or clerk,
used as a first name (*Old
French*).

Claud, Claude the English form
of **Claudius**.

Claudius lame (*Latin*); the Dutch
and German forms of **Claud**.

Clay a surname, meaning a
dweller in a place with clay
soil, used as a first name (*Old
English*); a diminutive form of
Clayton.

Clayton a placename and
surname, meaning place in or

with good clay, used as a first
name (*Old English*); a diminutive form is **Clay**.

Clement mild-tempered,
merciful (*Latin*); a diminutive
form is **Clem**.

Cliff a diminutive form of
Clifford, now used independently.

Clifford a surname, meaning
ford at a cliff, used as a first
name (*Old English*); a diminutive form is **Cliff**.

Clifton a placename, meaning
place on a cliff, used as a first
name (*Old English*).

Clint a diminutive form of
Clinton, used independently.

Clinton a placename and
surname, meaning settlement
on a hill, used as a first name; a
diminutive form is **Clint**.

Clive a surname, meaning at the
cliff, used as a first name (*Old
English*).

Clyde the name of a Scottish
river, meaning cleansing one,
used as a first name (*Scots
Gaelic*).

Col a diminutive form of
Colman, Columba.

Colby From the dark country
(*Norse*).

Cole a diminutive form of

Coleman, Colman, Nicholas; a surname, meaning swarthy or coal-black, used as a first name (*Old English*).

Coleman a surname, meaning swarthy man or servant of Nicholas, used as a first name (*Old English*).

Colin a diminutive form of **Nicholas**, used independently.

Colm dove (*Irish Gaelic/Latin*).

Colman, Colmán keeper of doves (*Irish Gaelic/Latin*); diminutive forms are **Col, Cole**.

Columba dove (*Latin*); a diminutive form is **Coly**.

Colyer a variant form of **Collier**.

Comyn bent (*Irish Gaelic*).

Con a diminutive form of **Conan, Connall, Connor, Conrad**.

Conan, Cónán little hound (*Irish Gaelic*); a diminutive form is **Con**.

Conn chief (*Celtic*).

Connall courageous (*Irish and Scots Gaelic*).

Connor high desire or will (*Irish Gaelic*).

Conrad able counsellor (*Germanic*); a diminutive form is **Con**.

Conroy wise (*Gaelic*).

Constant firm; faithful (*Latin*); a diminutive form is **Con**.

Constantine resolute; firm (*Latin*).

Conway a surname, of uncertain meaning—possibly yellow hound or head-smashing, used as a first name (*Irish Gaelic*); high or holy water (*Welsh*).

Cooper a surname, meaning barrel maker, used as a first name (*Old English*); a diminutive form is **Coop**.

Corbet, Corbett a surname, meaning raven, black-haired or raucousness, used as a first name (*Old French*).

Corey a surname, meaning god peace, used as a first name (*Irish Gaelic*).

Cormac, Cormack, Cormick charioteer (*Irish Gaelic*).

Cornelius origin uncertain, possibly horn-like, a Roman family name; a variant form is **Cornell**.

Cornell a surname, meaning Cornwall or a hill where corn is sold, used as a first name; a variant form of **Cornelius**.

Corwin friend of the heart (*Old French*).

Cosmo order, beauty (*Greek*).

Cradoc a variant form of **Caradoc**.

Craig a surname meaning crag, used as a first name (*Scots Gaelic*).

Crawford a placename and surname, meaning ford of the crows, used as a first name (*Old English*).

Creighton a surname, meaning rock or cliff place (*Old Welsh/Old English*) or border settlement (*Scots Gaelic*), used as a first name (*Old English*).

Crispin, Crispian having curly hair (*Latin*).

Crosbie, Crosby a placename and surname, meaning farm or village with crosses, used as a first name (*Old Norse*).

Cullan, Cullen a surname, meaning Cologne, used as a

first name (*Old French*); a placename, meaning at the back of the river, used as a first name (*Scots Gaelic*).

Curran a surname, of uncertain meaning—possibly resolute hero, used as a first name (*Irish Gaelic*).

Curt a variant form of **Kurt**; a diminutive form of **Curtis**.

Curtis a surname, meaning courteous, educated, used as a first name (*Old French*); a diminutive form is **Curt**.

Cuthbert famous bright (*Old English*).

Cy a diminutive form of **Cyrus**.

Cyril lordly (*Greek*).

Cyrus the sun (*Persian*); a diminutive form is **Cy**.

Dafydd a Welsh form of **David**.

Dai a Welsh diminutive form of David, formerly a name in its own right, meaning shining.

Dale a surname, meaning valley, used as a first name (*Old English*).

Daley a surname, meaning assembly, used as a first name (*Irish Gaelic*); a variant form is **Daly**.

Dallas a surname, meaning meadow resting place (*Scots Gaelic*) or dale house (*Old

English), used as a first name.

Dalton a surname, meaning dale farm, used as a first name (*Old English*).

Daly a variant of **Daley**.

Dalziel a placename and surname, meaning field of the sungleam, used as a first name (*Scots Gaelic*).

Damian, Damien taming (*Greek*).

Damon conqueror (*Greek*).

Dan a diminutive form of **Danby, Daniel**.

Dana a surname, of uncertain meaning—possibly Danish, used as a first name (*Old English*); *fem* form of **Dan, Daniel**.

Dandie a Scottish diminutive form of **Andrew**.

Dane a surname, meaning valley, used as a first name (*Old English*).

Daniel God is my judge (*Hebrew*); diminutive forms are **Dan, Dannie, Danny**.

Dannie, Danny diminutives of **Danby, Daniel**.

Dante steadfast (*Latin/Italian*).

Darby a variant form of Derby, a surname meaning a village where deer are seen, used as a first name (*Old Norse*); a

diminutive form of **Dermot, Diarmid** (*Irish Gaelic*).

Darell a variant form of **Darrell**.

Darien a South American placename also used as a first name.

Dario the Italian form of **Darius**.

Darius preserver (*Persian*).

Darnell a surname, meaning hidden nook, used as a first name (*Old English*).

Darrell, Darrel from a surname, meaning from Airelle in Normandy, used as a first name; variant forms are **Darell, Darryl, Daryl**.

Darren, Darin a surname, of unknown origin, used as a first name.

Daryl, Darryl variant forms of **Darrell**, also used as girls' names.

David beloved (*Hebrew*); diminutive forms are **Dave, Davie, Davy**.

Davie a diminutive form of **David**.

Davin a variant form of **Devin**.

Davis David's son (*Old English*).

Davy a diminutive form of **David**.

Dean a surname, meaning one who lives in a valley (*Old English*) or serving as a dean (*Old French*), used as a first

name; the anglicized form of
Dino.

Dearborn a surname, meaning
deer brook, used as a first
name (*Old English*).

Decimus tenth (*Latin*).

Declan the name, of unknown
meaning, of a 5th-century Irish
saint (*Irish Gaelic*).

Deinol charming (*Welsh*).

Dell a surname, meaning one
who lives in a hollow, used as
a first name; a diminutive form
of **Delmar**, etc.

Delmar of the sea (*Latin*).

Delwyn, Delwin neat and
blessed (*Welsh*).

Demetrius belonging to
Demeter, goddess of the
harvest, earth mother (*Greek*).

Dempsey a surname, meaning
proud descendant, used as a
first name (*Gaelic*).

Dempster a surname, meaning
judge, used as a first name,
formerly a feminine one (*Old
English*).

Den a diminutive form of **Denis,
Dennis, Denison, Denley,
Dennison, Denton, Denver,
Denzel, Denzell, Denzil**.

Denis, Dennis belonging to
Dionysus, the god of wine
(*Greek*).

Denison a variant form of
Dennison.

Dennison son of Dennis (*Old
English*); variant forms are
**Denison, Tennison,
Tennyson**.

Denton a surname, meaning
valley place, used as a first
name (*Old English*).

Denver a surname, meaning
Danes' crossing, used as a first
name (*Old English*).

Denzel, Denzell, Denzil a
surname, meaning stronghold,
used as a first name (*Celtic*).

Deon a variant form of **Dion**.

Derek, an English form of
Theoderic; variant forms are
Derrick, Derrik; a diminutive
form is **Derry**.

Dermot the anglicized form of
Diarmaid; a diminutive form is
Derry.

Derrick, Derrik variant forms of
Derek; a diminutive form is
Derry.

Derry the anglicized form of a
placename, meaning oak wood,
used as a first name (*Irish
Gaelic*); a diminutive form of
**Derek, Derrick, Derrik,
Dermot**.

Desmond a variant form of
Esmond (*Germanic*).

18

Devin, Devinn a surname, meaning poet, used as a first name (*Irish Gaelic*); a variant form is **Davin**.

Devlin fiercely brave (*Irish Gaelic*).

Dewey a Celtic form of **David**.

Dewi a Welsh form of **David**.

Dexter a surname, meaning (woman) dyer, used as a first name (*Old English*).

Diarmaid free of envy (*Irish Gaelic*); a variant form is **Diarmuid**; the anglicized form is **Dermot**.

Diarmid the Scottish Gaelic form of **Diarmaid**.

Diarmuid a variant form of **Diarmaid**.

Dick, Dickie, Dickon diminutive forms of **Richard.**

Dickson a surname, meaning son of Richard, used as a first name (*Old English*); a variant form is **Dixon**.

Dicky a diminutive form of **Richard**.

Digby a surname, meaning settlement at a ditch, used as a first name (*Old Norse*).

Dillon a surname of uncertain meaning, possibly destroyer, used as a first name (*Germanic/Irish Gaelic*).

Dion a shortened form of Dionysus, the god of wine (*Greek*); a variant form is **Deon**.

Dirk the Dutch form of **Derek**; a diminutive form of **Theodoric**.

Dixon a variant form of **Dickson**.

Dolan a variant form of **Doolan**.

Dominic, Dominick belonging to the lord (*Latin*); a diminutive form is **Dom**.

Don a diminutive form of **Donal, Donald, Donall**.

Donal anglicized forms of **Dónal**; a variant form is **Donall**; diminutive forms are **Don, Donnie, Donny**.

Dónal an Irish Gaelic form of **Donald**.

Donald proud chief (*Scots Gaelic*); diminutive forms are **Don, Donnie, Donny**.

Donall a variant form of **Donal**.

Donnie, Donny diminutive forms of **Donal, Donald, Donall**.

Doolan a surname, meaning black defiance, used as a first name (*Irish Gaelic*); a variant form is **Dolan**.

Doran a surname, meaning stranger or exile, used as a first name (*Irish Gaelic*).

Dorian Dorian man, one of a Hellenic people who invaded Greece in the 2nd century BC (*Greek*); its use as a first name was probably invented by Oscar Wilde for his novel, *The Picture of Dorian Gray*.

Dorward a variant form of **Durward**.

Dougal, Dougall black stranger (*Gaelic*); variant forms are **Dugal, Dugald**; diminutive forms are **Doug, Dougie, Duggie**.

Douglas a surname and placename, meaning black water, used as a first name (*Scots Gaelic*); diminutive forms are **Doug, Dougie, Duggie**.

Doyle an Irish Gaelic form of **Dougal**.

Drake a first name meaning dragon or standard bearer, used as first name (*Old English*).

Drew a Scottish diminutive form of **Andrew**; a surname, meaning trusty (*Germanic*) or lover (*Old French*), used as a first name.

Driscoll, Driscol a surname, meaning interpreter, used as a first name (*Irish Gaelic*).

Druce a surname meaning from Eure or Rieux in France (*Old French*), or a sturdy lover, used as a first name (*Celtic*).

Drummond a surname, meaning ridge, used as a first name.

Drury a surname, meaning dear one, used as a first name (*Old French*).

Dryden a surname, meaning dry valley, used as a first name (*Old English*).

Duane dark (*Irish Gaelic*); a variant forms is **Dwane, Dwayne**.

Dudley a placename, meaning Dudda's clearing, used as a first name (*Old English*).

Dugal, Dugald variant forms of **Dougal**; a diminutive form is **Duggie**.

Duggie a diminutive form of **Dougal, Dougald, Douglas, Dugal, Dugald**.

Duke the title of an English aristocrat used as a first name; a diminutive form of **Marmaduke**.

Duncan brown chief (*Gaelic*); a diminutive form is **Dunc**.

Dunn, Dunne a surname, meaning dark-skinned, used as a first name (*Old English*).

Dunstan brown hill stone (*Old English*).

Durand, Durant a surname,

meaning enduring or obstinate, used as a first name (*Old French*).

Durward a surname meaning doorkeeper or gatekeeper, used as a first name (*Old English*); a variant form is **Dorward**.

Durwin dear friend (*Old English*); a diminutive form is **Durwyn**.

Dustin a surname, of uncertain meaning—possibly of Dionysus, used as a first name.

Dwayne a variant form of **Duane, Dwane**.

Dwight a surname, meaning Thor's stone, used as a first name (*Old Norse*).

Dyfan ruler (*Welsh*).

Dylan sea (*Welsh*).

Eachan, Eachann, Eacheann horse (*Scots Gaelic*).

Eamon, Eamonn an Irish Gaelic form of **Edmund**.

Earl, Earle an English title, meaning nobleman, used as a first name (*Old English*); a variant form is **Erle**.

Eaton a surname, meaning river or island farm, used as a first name (*Old English*).

Eb a diminutive form of **Eben, Ebenezer**, etc.

Eben stone (*Hebrew*); a diminutive form is **Eb**.

Ebenezer stone of help (*Hebrew*); diminutive forms are **Eb, Eben**.

Ed a diminutive form of **Edbert, Edgar, Edmund, Edward, Edwin**.

Edan a Scottish form of **Aidan**.

Eddie, Eddy diminutive forms of **Edbert, Edgar, Edmund, Edward, Edwin**.

Eden pleasantness (*Hebrew*); a surname, meaning blessed helmet, sometimes used as a first name.

Edgar prosperity spear (*Old English*); diminutive forms are **Ed, Eddie, Eddy, Ned, Neddie, Neddy**.

Edmund prosperity defender (*Old English*).

Edryd restoration (*Welsh*).

Edward guardian of happiness (*Old English*); diminutive forms are **Ed, Eddie, Eddy, Ned, Ted, Teddy**.

Edwin prosperity friend (*Old English*).

Ehren Honourable one (*Germanic*).

Eilir butterfly (*Welsh*).

Eldridge wise adviser (*Old English*).

Elfed autumn (*Welsh*).

Elgan bright circle (*Welsh*).

Eli a diminutive form of **Elias, Elijah, Eliezer**; a variant form is **Ely**.

Elias a variant form of **Elijah**; a diminutive form is **Eli**.

Elijah Jehovah is my God (*Hebrew*); a diminutive form is **Lije**.

Eliot a variant form of **Elliot**.

Elis a Welsh form of **Elias**.

Elisha God is salvation (*Hebrew*).

Elliot, Elliot a surname, from a French diminutive form of **Elias**, now frequently used as a first name.

Ellis a surname, a Middle English form of **Elias**, used as a first name.

Ellison a surname, meaning son of Elias, used as a first name (*Old English*).

Elmer noble; excellent (*Germanic*)

Elmore a surname, meaning river bank with elms, used as a first name (*Old English*).

Elroy a variant form of **Leroy**.

Elton a surname, meaning settlement of Ella, used as a first name (*Old English*).

Elvin a surname, meaning elf or noble friend, used as a first name (*Old English*); a variant form is **Elwin**.

Elvis wise one (*Norse*).

Elvy a variant form of **Elvey**.

Elwin a variant form of **Elvin**; white brow (*Welsh*); a variant form is **Elwyn**.

Emery a variant form of **Amory**.

Emil of a noble Roman family the origin of whose name, *Aemilius*, is uncertain.

Émile the French form of **Emil**.

Emlyn origin uncertain, possibly from **Emil** (*Welsh*).

Emmanuel God with us (*Hebrew*); a variant form is **Immanuel**; a diminutive form is **Manny**.

Emmet, Emmett, Emmot, Emmott industrious (*Old English/Germanic*).

Emory a variant form of **Amory**.

Emrys a Welsh form of **Ambrose**.

Emyr a Welsh form of **Honorius**.

Engelbert bright angel (*Germanic*).

Ennis chief one (*Gaelic*).

Enoch dedication (*Hebrew*).

Enos man (*Hebrew*).

Eoghan an Irish Gaelic form of **Eugene**.

Eoin an Irish form of **John**.

Ephraim fruitful (*Hebrew*); a diminutive form is **Eph**.

Erasmus lovely; worthy of love (*Greek*); a diminutive form is **Ras, Rasmus**.

Erastus beloved (*Greek*); diminutive forms are **Ras, Rastus**.

Eric rich; brave; powerful (*Old English*); a variant form is **Erik**.

Erik a variant form of **Eric**.

Erland stranger (*Old Norse*).

Erle a variant form of **Earl**.

Ern a diminutive form of **Ernest**.

Ernest earnestness (*Germanic*); diminutive forms are **Ern, Ernie**.

Erskine a placename and surname, meaning projecting height, used as a first name (*Scots Gaelic*).

Eryl watcher (*Welsh*).

Esau hairy (*Hebrew*).

Esmond divine protection (*Old English*).

Ethan firm (*Hebrew*).

Euan a variant form of **Ewan**.

Eugen the German form of **Eugene**.

Eugene well-born; noble (*Greek*); a diminutive form is **Gene**.

Eurig, Euros gold (*Welsh*).

Eustace rich (*Greek*); diminutive forms are **Stacey, Stacy**.

Evan young warrior (*Celtic*).

Evelyn the English surname used as a first name.

Everard strong boar (*Germanic*).

Everley Field of the wild boar (*Old English*).

Ewan, Ewen Irish and Scots Gaelic forms of **Owen**; a Scottish form of **Eugene**; a variant form is **Euan**.

Ewart an Old French variant of **Edward**; a surname, meaning herd of ewes used as a first name (*Old English*).

Ezra help (*Hebrew*).

Fabian the anglicized form of the Roman family name *Fabianus*, derived from *Fabius*, from *faba*, bean (*Latin*).

Farnall, Farnell a surname, meaning fern hill, used as a first name (*Old English*); variant forms are **Fernald, Fernall**.

Farquhar friendly man (*Scots Gaelic*).

Farrell warrior (*Irish Gaelic*).

Felix happy (*Latin*).

Fenton a placename and surname, meaning a place in marshland or fens, used as a first name (*Old English*).

Ferdinand peace bold (*Germanic*); diminutive forms are **Ferd, Ferdy**.

Fergal man of strength (*Irish Gaelic*); diminutive forms are **Fergie, Fergy**.

Fergie a diminutive form of **Fergal, Fergus, Ferguson**.

Fergus vigorous man (*Irish/Scots Gaelic*); diminutive forms are **Fergie, Fergy**.

Ferguson, Fergusson a surname, meaning son of Fergus, used as a first name; diminutive forms are **Fergie, Fergy**.

Fergy a variant form of **Fergie**.

Fernald, Fernall variant forms of **Farnall, Farnell**.

Fidelis faithful (*Latin*); a diminutive form is **Fid**.

Fielding a surname, meaning dweller in a field, used as a first name (*Old English*).

Findlay a variant form of **Finlay**.

Fingal white stranger (*Scots Gaelic*).

Finlay, Finley fair warrior or calf (*Scots Gaelic*); a variant form is **Findlay**.

Finn fair, white (*Irish Gaelic*); a variant form is **Fionn**.

Fionn a variant form of **Finn**.

Fitz son (*Old French*); a diminutive form of names beginning with Fitz-.

Fitzgerald a surname, meaning son of Gerald, used as a first name (*Old French*); a diminutive form is **Fitz**.

Fitzhugh a surname, meaning son of Hugh, used as a first name (*Old French*); a diminutive form is **Fitz**.

Fitzpatrick a surname, meaning son of Patrick, used as a first name (*Old French*); a diminutive form is **Fitz**.

Fitzroy a surname, meaning (illegitimate) son of the king, used as a first name (*Old French*); a diminutive form is **Fitz**.

Flann red-haired (*Irish Gaelic*).

Flannan red-complexioned (*Irish Gaelic*).

Fleming a surname, meaning man from Flanders, used as a first name (*Old French*).

Fletcher a surname meaning arrow-maker, used as a first name (*Old French*).

Flinn a variant form of **Flynn**.

Flint stream, brook (*Old English*).

Floyd a variant form of the surname Lloyd used as a first name.

Flynn a surname, meaning son of the red-haired one, used as a first name (*Scots Gaelic*); a variant form is **Flinn**.

Forbes a placename and surname, meaning fields or district, used as a first name (*Scots Gaelic*).

Ford the English word for a crossing place of a river, now used as a first name (*Old English*).

Forrest, Forrestt a surname, meaning forest, used as a first name (*Old French*).

Forrester, Forster a surname, meaning forester, used as a first name (*Old French*).

Foster a surname, meaning forester or cutler (*Old French*) or foster parent (*Old English*), used as a first name.

Fran a diminutive form of **Francis**.

Francis free (*Germanic*); diminutive forms are **Fran, Frank, Francie**.

Frank Frenchman (*Old French*) a diminutive form of **Francis, Franklin**; diminutive forms are **Frankie, Franky**.

Franklin, Franklen, Franklyn a surname, meaning freeholder, used as a first name (*Old French*); diminutive forms are **Frank, Frankie, Franky**.

Fraser, Frasier a Scottish surname, meaning from Frisselle or Fresel in France— possibly strawberry, used as a first name (*French*); variant forms are **Frazer, Frazier**.

Frazer, Frazier variant forms of **Fraser**.

Frederick, Frederic abounding in peace; peaceful ruler (*Germanic*); diminutive forms

are **Fred, Freddie, Freddy**.

Fulton a surname, meaning muddy place, used as a first name (*Old English*).

Fyfe, Fyffe a surname, meaning from Fife, used as a first name.

Gabe diminutive form of **Gabriel**.

Gabriel strength of God; man of God; in the Bible one of the archangels (*Hebrew*); a diminutive form is **Gabe**.

Galen the anglicized form of the Roman family name *Galenus*, calmer (*Latin*).

Gallagher a surname, meaning foreign helper, used as a first name (*Irish Gaelic*).

Galloway a placename and surname, meaning stranger Gaels, used as a first name (*Old Welsh*).

Galvin bright, white (*Irish Gaelic*).

Gamaliel recompense of God (*Hebrew*).

Gareth old man (*Welsh*);

diminutive forms are **Gary, Garry**; a variant form is **Garth**.

Garfield a surname, meaning triangular piece of open land, used as a first name (*Old English*).

Garnet, Garnett a surname, meaning pomegranate, used as a first name (*Old French*).

Garrard a variant form of **Gerard**.

Garret, Garrett the Irish Gaelic form of **Gerard**; a variant form of **Garrard**.

Garrison a surname, meaning son of Garret, used as a first name (*Old English*).

Garry a variant form of **Gary**; a placename, meaning rough (water), used as a first name (*Scots Gaelic*).

Garth a surname, meaning garden or paddock, used as a first name (*Old Norse*); a variant form of **Gareth**.

Garve a placename, meaning rough place, used as a first name (*Scots Gaelic*).

Gary spear carrier (*Germanic*); a diminutive form of **Gareth**; a variant form is **Garry**.

Gaston stranger, guest (*Germanic*); from Gascony (*Old French*).

Gavin an anglicized form of **Gawain**.

Gawain white hawk (*Welsh*).

Gaylord a surname, meaning brisk noble man, used as a first name (*Old French*).

Gene a diminutive form of **Eugene**, now used independently.

Geoffrey a variant form of **Jeffrey**; a diminutive form is **Geoff**.

George a landholder; husbandman (*Germanic*); diminutive forms are **Geordie, Georgie, Georgy**.

Geraint old man (*Welsh*).

Gerald strong with the spear (*Germanic*); diminutive forms are **Gerrie, Gerry, Jerry**.

Gerard firm spear (*Old Ger-man*); variant forms are **Garrard, Garratt, Gerrard**; diminutive forms are **Gerrie, Gerry, Jerry**.

Germain brother (*Latin*).

Gerrie, Gerry diminutive forms of **Gerald, Gerard.**

Gershom an exile (*Hebrew*).

Gervaise a variant form of **Gervase**.

Gervase spearman (*Germanic*); variant forms are **Gervaise, Jarvis, Jervis**.

Gethin dusky (*Welsh*).

Gibson a surname, meaning son of Gilbert, used as a first name (*Old English*).

Gideon a destroyer (*Hebrew*).

Giffard, Gifford a surname, meaning bloated (*Old French*) or gift (*Germanic*), used a first name.

Gil a diminutive form of **Gilbert, Gilchrist, Giles**.

Gilbert yellow-bright; famous (*Germanic*); a diminutive form is **Gil**.

Gilchrist servant of Christ (*Scots Gaelic*); a diminutive form is **Gil**.

Giles a kid (*Greek*); a diminutive form is **Gil**.

Gillespie a surname, meaning the servant of a bishop, also used as a first name (*Scots Gaelic*).

Gillmore a variant form of **Gilmore**.

Gilmore, Gilmour a surname, meaning servant of St Mary, used as a first name (*Scots Gaelic*); a variant form is **Gillmore**.

Gilroy a surname, meaning servant of the red haired one, used as a first name (*Gaelic*).

Gladwin a surname, meaning glad friend, used as a first name (*Old English*).

Glen the surname, meaning a valley, used as a first name (*Scots Gaelic*); a variant form is **Glenn**.

Glendon From the fortress in the Glen (*Celtic*).

Glenn a variant form of **Glen**, now also used as a feminine name.

Glyn valley (*Welsh*); a variant form is **Glynn**.

Glynn a variant form of **Glyn**.

Goddard pious; virtuous (*Old German*).

Godfrey at peace with God (*Germanic*).

Godwin God's friend (*Old English*).

Goldwin Golden friend (*Old English*).

Goliath mighty warrior (*Hebrew*).

Goodwin a surname, meaning good friend, used as a first name; (*Old English*).

Gordon a surname, meaning great hill, used as a first name (*Scots Gaelic*).

Grady a surname, meaning noble, used as a first name (*Irish Gaelic*).

Graham, Grahame, Graeme a Scottish surname, 'meaning one who lives by the grey land', used as a first name (*Celtic*).

Granger a surname, meaning farmer or bailiff, used as a first name (*Old English*).

Grant a surname, meaning large, used as a first name (*Norman French*).

Granville large town (*Old French*).

Gray a surname, meaning grey-haired, used as a first name (*Old English*); a variant form is **Grey**.

Gregor a Scots form of **Gregory**.

Gregory watchful; (*Greek*); a diminutive form is **Greg**.

Gresham a surname, meaning grazing meadow, used as a first name (*Old English*).

Greville a surname, meaning

from Gréville in France, used as
a first name.

Grier a surname, a contracted
form of **Gregor**, used as a first
name.

Griff a diminutive form of
Griffin, Griffith.

Griffin a Latinized form of
Griffith; a diminutive form is
Griff.

Griffith an anglicized form of
Gruffydd; a diminutive form is
Griff.

Grover a surname, meaning
from a grove of trees, used as a
first name (*Old English*).

Gruffydd powerful chief
(*Welsh*).

Gus a diminutive form of **Angus,
Augustus, Gustave**.

Gustave staff of the Goths (*Swedish*); a diminutive form is **Gus**.

Guthrie a surname, meaning
windy, used as a first name
(*Scots Gaelic*).

Guy a leader (*German-French*).

Gwillym, Gwilym Welsh forms
of **William**.

Gwyn, Gwynn fair, blessed
(*Welsh*); diminutive forms are
Gwyn, Guin.

Gwynfor fair lord (*Welsh*).

Haddan, Hadden, Haddon a
surname, meaning heathery
hill, used as a first name (*Old
English*).

Hadley a surname, meaning
heathery hill or heathery
meadow, used as a first name
(*Old English*).

Hadrian a variant form of
Adrian.

Hagan young Hugh (*Irish*

Gaelic); thorn bush or thorn
fence (*Germanic*).

Haig a first name, meaning one
who lives in an enclosure, used
as a first name (*Old English*).

Hal a diminutive form of
Halbert, Henry.

Halbert brilliant hero (*Old
English*); a diminutive form is
Hal.

Hale a surname, meaning from

the hall, used as a surname
(*Old English*).

Haley a variant form of **Hayley**.

Halford a surname, meaning
from a ford in a hollow, used
as a first name (*Old English*).

Haliwell a variant form of
Halliwell.

Hall a surname, meaning one
who lives at a manor house,
used as a first name (*Old
English*).

Hallam a surname, meaning at
the hollow (*Old English*), or a
placename, meaning at the
rocky place (*Old Norse*), used
as a first name.

Halliwell a surname, meaning
one who lives by the holy well,
used as a first name (*Old
English*); a variant form is
Haliwell.

Halton a surname, meaning from
the lookout hill, used as a first
name (*Old English*).

Hamar strong man (*Old Norse*).

Hamilton a surname, meaning
farm in broken country, used as
a first name (*Old English*).

Hamish a Scots Gaelic form of
James.

Hammond a surname, meaning
belonging to Hamon, used as a
first name (*Old English*).

Hamon great protection (*Old
English*).

Hanford a surname, meaning
rocky ford or ford with cocks,
used as a first name (*Old
English*).

Hank a diminutive form of
Henry.

Hanley a surname, meaning
from the high meadow or hill,
used as a first name (*Old
English*).

Hannibal grace of Baal (*Punic*).

Hans a diminutive form of
Johann.

Hansel gift from God (*Scandinavian*).

Harbert a variant form of
Herbert.

Harden a surname, meaning the
valley of the hare, used as a
first name (*Old English*).

Hardie, Hardey variant forms of
Hardy.

Harding a surname, meaning
brave warrior, used as a first
name (*Old English*).

Hardy a surname, meaning bold
and daring, used as a first name
(*Germanic*); variant forms are
Hardey, Hardie.

Harford a surname, meaning
stags' ford, used as a first name
(*Old English*).

Hargrave, Hargreave, Hargreaves a surname, meaning from the hare grove, used as a first name (*Old English*).

Harlan, Harland a surname, meaning rocky land, used as a first name (*Old English*).

Harley a surname, meaning from the hare meadow or hill, used as a first name (*Old English*).

Harlow a placename and surname, meaning fortified hill, used as a first name (*Old English*).

Harold a champion; general of an army (*Old English*).

Harper a surname, meaning harp player or maker, used as a first name (*Old English*).

Harris, Harrison surnames, meaning son of Harold or Harry, used as first names (*Old English*)

Harry a diminutive form of **Henry**, also used independently.

Hart a surname, meaning hart deer, used as a first name (*Old English*).

Hartford a placename and surname, meaning ford of the deer, or army ford, used as a first name (*Old English*);

a variant form is **Hertford**.

Hartley a surname, meaning clearing with stags, used as a first name (*Old English*).

Hartmann, Hartman strong and brave (*Germanic*).

Hartwell a surname, meaning stags' stream, used as a first name (*Old English*).

Harvey, Harvie a surname, meaning battle worthy, used as a first name (*Breton Gaelic*); a variant form is **Hervey**.

Haslett, Hazlitt variant forms of **Hazlett**.

Hayden, Haydon a surname, meaning heather hill or hay hill, used as a first name (*Old English*).

Hayley a surname, meaning hay clearing, used as a first name (*Old English*); a variant form is **Haley**.

Hayward a surname, meaning supervisor of enclosures, used as a first name (*Old English*); a variant form is **Heyward**.

Haywood a surname, meaning fenced forest, used as a first name (*Old English*); a variant form is **Heywood**.

Heath a surname, meaning heathland, used as a first name (*Old English*).

Heathcliff, Heathcliffe dweller by the heather cliff (*Old English*).

Hector holding fast (*Greek*).

Hefin summery (*Welsh*).

Henry the head or chief of a house (*Germanic*); diminutive forms are **Harry, Hal, Hank**.

Herbert army bright (*Old English*); a variant form is **Harbert**; diminutive forms are **Herb, Herbie**.

Hercules glory of Hera (the Latin form of the name of Herakles, the Greek hero, son of Zeus and stepson of Hera).

Herman, Hermann warrior (*Germanic*).

Hermes in Greek mythology, the messenger of the gods, with winged feet. His counterpart in Roman mythology is Mercury.

Herrick a surname, meaning powerful army, used as a first name (*Old Norse*).

Hertford a variant form of **Hartford**.

Hervey a variant form of **Harvey**.

Hesketh a surname, meaning horse track, used as a first name (*Old Norse*).

Hew a Welsh form of **Hugh**.

Hewett, Hewit a surname,

meaning little Hugh or cleared place, used as a first name (*Old English*).

Heyward a variant form of **Hayward**.

Heywood a variant form of **Haywood**.

Hezekiah strength of the Lord (*Hebrew*).

Hi a diminutive form of **Hiram, Hyram**.

Hieronymus the Latin and German forms of **Jerome**.

Hilary, Hillary cheerful; merry (*Latin*); also used as a girl's name.

Hilton a surname, meaning from the hill farm, used as a first name (*Old English*); a variant form is **Hylton**.

Hiram brother of the exalted one (*Hebrew*); a variant form is **Hyram**; a diminutive form is **Hi**.

Hobart a variant form of **Hubert**.

Hogan youthful (*Irish Gaelic*).

Holbert, Holbird variant forms of **Hulbert**.

Holbrook a surname, meaning brook in the valley, used as a first name (*Old English*).

Holcomb, Holcombe a surname, meaning deep valley,

used as a first name (*Old English*).

Holden a surname, meaning from the deep valley, used as a first name (*Old English*).

Hollis a surname, meaning dweller near holly trees, used as a first name (*Old English*).

Holmes a surname, meaning an island in a river, used as a first name (*Old English*).

Holt a surname, meaning a wood or forest, used as a first name (*Old English*).

Homer uncertain, possibly hostage (*Greek*); the name of the Greek epic poet of the first millennium BC.

Horace, Horatio origin uncertain, possibly a family name *Horatius* (*Latin*).

Horton a surname, meaning muddy place, used as a first name (*Old English*).

Houghton a surname, meaning place in an enclosure, used as a first name (*Old English*); a variant form is **Hutton**.

Houston, Houstun a surname, meaning Hugh's place, used as a first name (*Old English*).

Howard a surname, meaning mind strong, used as a first name (*Germanic*).

Howe a surname, meaning high one (*Germanic*) or hill (*Old English*) used as a first name.

Howel, Howell anglicized forms of **Hywel**.

Hubert mind bright (*Germanic*); a variant surname form is **Hobart**.

Hudson a surname, meaning son of little Hugh, used as a first name (*Old English*).

Hugh mind; spirit; (*Germanic*).

Hugo the Latin, German, and Spanish form of **Hugh**, now used independently as an English-language form.

Hulbert, Hulburd, Hulburt a surname, meaning brilliant, gracious, used as a first name (*Germanic*); variant forms are **Holbert, Holbird**.

Humbert bright warrior (*Germanic*).

Humphrey, Humphry giant peace (*Old English*); diminutive forms are **Hump, Humph**.

Hunt, Hunter surnames, meaning hunter, used as first names (*Old English*).

Huntley, Huntly a surname, meaning hunter's meadow, used as a first name (*Old English*).

Hurley sea tide (*Gaelic*).

Hutton a variant form of **Houghton**.

Huw a Welsh variant form of **Hugh**.

Huxley a surname, meaning Hugh's meadow, used as a first name (*Old English*).

Hyam man of life (*Hebrew*); a variant form is **Hyman**; diminutive forms are **Hi, Hy**.

Hyde a surname, meaning a hide (measurement unit) of land, used as a first name (*Old English*).

Hylton a variant form of **Hilton**.

Hyman a variant form of **Hyam**.

Hyram a variant form of **Hiram**; diminutive forms are **Hi, Hy**.

Hywel, Hywell sound; whole (*Welsh*); anglicized forms are **Howel, Howell**.

Iain the Scots Gaelic form of **John**.

Ian an anglicized form of **Iain**.

Ichabod inglorious (*Hebrew*).

Idris fiery lord (*Welsh*).

Iestyn the Welsh form of **Justin**.

Ieuan, Ifan Welsh forms of **John**; a variant form is **Iwan**.

Ifor a Welsh form of **Ivor**.

Ignatius from *ignis*, fire (*Greek*).

Igor the Russian form of **Ivor**.

Ike a diminutive form of **Isaac**.

Immanuel a variant form of **Emmanuel**; a diminutive form is **Manny**.

Inge a diminutive form of **Ingemar**.

Ingemar, Ingmar famous son of Ing (*Old Norse*); a diminutive form is **Inge**.

Ingram a surname, meaning raven angel (*Germanic*) or river meadow (*Old English*), used as a first name.

Inigo a Spanish form of **Ignatius**, now used as an English-language form.

Innes, Inness a surname, meaning island, used as a first name (*Scots Gaelic*).

Iorwerth handsome nobleman (*Welsh*); diminutive forms are **Iolo, Iolyn**.

Ira watchful (*Hebrew*).

Irvine, Irving a surname, meaning fresh or green river, used as a first name (*Celtic*).

Irwin a surname, meaning friend of boars, used as a first name (*Old English*).

Isaac laughter (*Hebrew*); a variant form is **Izaak**; a diminutive form is **Ike**.

Isaiah salvation of Jehovah (*Hebrew*).

Isham a surname, meaning home on the water, used as a first name (*Old English*).

Isidore gift of Isis (*Greek*).

Israel a soldier of God ruling with the Lord (*Hebrew*); a diminutive form is **Izzy**.

Ivan the Russian form of **John**.

Ives a surname, meaning son of Ive (yew), used as a first name (*Germanic*).

Ivo the Welsh form of **Yves**.

Ivor yew army (*Old Norse*).

Iwan a variant form of **Ieuan**.

Izaak a variant form of **Isaac**.

Izzie, Izzy diminutive forms of **Israel**.

Jabal guide (*Hebrew*).

Jabez causing pain (*Hebrew*).

Jack a diminutive form of **John**, used independently; diminutive forms are **Jackie, Jacky**.

Jackie, Jacky a diminutive form of **Jack, John**.

Jackson a surname, meaning son of Jack, used as a first name.

Jacob supplanter (*Hebrew*); a diminutive form is **Jake**.

Jacques the French form of **Jacob, James**.

Jago a Cornish form of **James**.

Jairus he will enlighten (*Hebrew*).

Jake a diminutive form of **Jacob**, now used independently.

Jamal beauty (*Arabic*).

James a Christian form of **Jacob**; diminutive forms are **Jamie, Jem, Jim, Jimmy**.

Jamie a diminutive form of **James**, now used independently, often as a girl's name.

Jan a diminutive form of **John**; the Dutch form of **John**.

Japheth extension (*Hebrew*).

Jared servant (*Hebrew*).

Jarvis a surname form of **Gervase** used as a first name; a variant form is **Jervis**.

Jason healer (*Greek*); in Greek mythology, the hero who led the Argonauts.

Jasper treasure master (*Persian*).

Javan clay (*Hebrew*).

Javier a Portuguese and Spanish form of **Xavier**.

Jay a surname, meaning jay, the bird, used as a first name (*Old French*); a variant form is **Jaye**; a diminutive form for names beginning with *J*.

Jedidiah beloved of the Lord (*Hebrew*); a diminutive form is **Jed**.

Jefferson a surname, meaning son of Jeffrey or Geoffrey, used as a first name (*Old English*).

Jeffrey, Jeffery district or traveller peace (*Germanic*); a variant form is **Geoffrey**; a diminutive form is **Jeff**.

Jehudi Jewish (*Hebrew*); a variant form is **Yehudi**.

Jem, Jemmie, Jemmy diminutive forms of **James**.

Jeremy, Jeremiah Jehovah has appointed (*Hebrew*); a diminutive form is **Jerry**.

Jerome holy name (*Greek*); a diminutive form is **Jerry**.

Jerry a diminutive form of **Gerald, Gerard, Jeremy, Jerome**, used independently.

Jervis a variant form of **Jarvis**.

Jesse wealth (*Hebrew*).

Jethro (*Hebrew*) superiority.

Jim, Jimmie, Jimmy diminutive forms of **James**.

Jo a diminutive form of **Joab, Joachim, Joseph**.

Joab Jehovah is Father (*Hebrew*).

Joachim God has established (*Hebrew*).

Job one persecuted (*Hebrew*).

Jocelyn, Jocelin little Goth (*Germanic*); diminutive forms are **Jos, Joss**.

Jock, Jockie a diminutive form of **John**.

Joe, Joey diminutive forms of **Joseph**.

Joel Jehovah is God (*Hebrew*).

John Jehovah has been gracious (*Hebrew*); diminutive forms are **Jack, Jackie, Jan, Jock, Johnnie, Johnny**.

Jolyon a variant form of **Julian**.

Jon a variant form of **John**; a diminutive form of **Jonathan, Jonathon**.

Jonah, Jonas dove (*Hebrew*).

Jonathan, Jonathon Jehovah

gave (*Hebrew*); a diminutive form is **Jon**.

Jordan flowing down (*Hebrew*); diminutive forms are **Jud, Judd**.

Jos a diminutive form of **Joseph, Joshua**; a diminutive form of **Jocelyn, Jocelin**.

Joseph God shall add (*Hebrew*); diminutive forms are **Jo, Joe, Joey, Jos**.

Josh a diminutive form of **Joshua**, used independently.

Joshua Jehovah is salvation (*Hebrew*); a diminutive form is **Josh**.

Josiah, Josias Jehovah supports (*Hebrew*).

Joss a diminutive form of **Jocelyn, Jocelin**.

Juan the Spanish form of **John**, now used as an English-language form.

Jud, Judd diminutive forms of **Jordan**, used independently.

Judah confession (*Hebrew*); a diminutive form is **Jude**.

Jude a diminutive form of **Judah**.

Julian sprung from or belonging to Julius (*Latin*); a variant form is **Jolyon**.

Julien the French form of **Julian**.

Julius downy-bearded (*Greek*).

Justin just one (*Latin*); variant forms are **Justinian, Justus**.

Kane a surname, meaning warrior, used as a first name (*Irish Gaelic*).

Karl a German form of **Charles**.

Karr a variant form of **Kerr**.

Kasper the German form of **Jasper**.

Kavan a variant form of **Cavan**.

Kay, Kaye giant (*Scots Gaelic*).

Kean, Keane anglicized forms of **Cian**.

Keefe noble (*Irish Gaelic*).

Keegan a surname, meaning son of Egan, used as a first name (*Irish Gaelic*).

Keenan a surname, meaning little ancient one, used as a first name (*Irish Gaelic*).

Keir a surname, meaning swarthy, used as a first name (*Scots Gaelic*).

Keith a placename and surname, meaning wood, used as a first name (*Celtic*).

Kelsey a surname, meaning victory, used as a first name (*Old English*).

Kelvin the name of a Scottish river, meaning narrow water, used as a first name (*Scots Gaelic*).

Kemp a surname, meaning warrior (*Old English*) or athlete (*Middle English*), used as a first name.

Ken a diminutive form of **Kendall, Kendrick, Kenelm, Kennard, Kennedy, Kenneth**.

Kendall, Kendal, Kendell a surname, meaning valley of the holy river, used as a first name (*Celtic/Old English*); a diminutive form is **Ken**.

Kendrick a surname, meaning hero, used as a first name (*Welsh*); a variant form is **Kenrick**; a diminutive form is **Ken**.

Kenelm royal helmet (*Germanic*) a diminutive form is **Ken**.

Kennard a surname, meaning strong royal, used as a first name (*Germanic*) a diminutive form is **Ken**.

Kennedy a surname, meaning helmeted or ugly head, used as a first name (*Gaelic*); a diminutive form is **Ken**.

Kennet a Scandinavian form of Kenneth; diminutive forms are **Ken, Kent**.

Kenneth fire-born; handsome (*Gaelic*); diminutive forms are **Ken, Kennie, Kenny**.

Kennie, Kenny diminutive forms of **Kenneth** and other names beginning with Ken-.

Kenrick a variant form of **Kendrick**.

Kent a surname, meaning from the county of Kent (meaning border), used as a first name (*Celtic*); a diminutive form of **Kennet, Kenton**.

Kenton a surname, meaning settlement on the river Kenn, or royal place, used as a first name (*Old English*); diminutive forms are **Ken, Kent**.

Kenyon white-haired (*Gaelic*); a surname, meaning mound of Ennion, used as a first name (*Welsh*).

Kermit son of Diarmid (*Gaelic*).

Kern dark one (*Gaelic*).

Kerr a Scottish form of the surname **Carr**, sometimes used as a first name; a variant form is **Karr**.

Kester a diminutive form of **Christopher**.

Kevin, Kevan comely, loved (*Irish Gaelic*); a diminutive form is **Kev**.

Kieran an anglicized form of **Ciaran**.

Kiernan a variant form of **Tiernan**.

Kingsley a surname, meaning king's meadow, used as a first name (*Old English*).

Kingston a placename and surname, meaning king's farm, used as a first name (*Old English*).

Kinsey a surname, meaning royal victor, used as a first name (*Old English*).

Kirby a surname, meaning church village or farm, used as a first name (*Old Norse*).

Kirk a surname, meaning one who lives near a church, used as a first name (*Old Norse*).

Kit a diminutive form of **Christopher, Kristopher**.

Kurt a diminutive form of **Conrad**, now used independently; a variant form is **Curt**.

Kyle narrow (*Scots Gaelic*); the name of a region of southwest Scotland used as a first name.

Lacey a surname, meaning from Lassy in the Calvados region of Normandy, used as a first name (*Old French*).

Lachlan from the land of lakes (*Scots Gaelic*).

Laing a variant form of **Lang**.

Laird a Scots form of the surname Lord, meaning master, landowner (*Old English*), used as a first name.

Lambert illustrious with landed possessions (*Germanic*).

Lamond, Lamont a surname, meaning law giver, used as a first name (*Old Norse*).

Lance land (*Germanic*); a diminutive form of **Lancelot**.

Lancelot a little lance or warrior; or a servant (*French*); a diminutive form is **Lance**.

Lander, Landor variant forms of the surname **Lavender**.

Lane a surname, meaning narrow road, lane, used as a first name (*Old English*).

Lang a Scottish form of the surname Long, meaning tall or long, used as a first name (*Old English*); a variant form is **Laing**.

Langford a surname, meaning long ford, used as a first name (*Old English*).

Langley a surname, meaning long meadow, used as a first name (*Old English*).

Larry a diminutive form of **Laurence, Lawrence**.

Lars a Scandinavian form of **Laurence**.

Larsen, Larson son of Lars (*Scandinavian*).

Latham, Lathom a surname, meaning barns, used as a first name (*Old Norse*).

Latimer a surname, meaning interpreter, used as a first name (*Old French*).

Laurence from Laurentium in

Italy, place of laurels (*Latin*); a variant form is **Lawrence**; diminutive forms are **Larry, Laurie**.

Laurie a diminutive form of **Laurence**; a surname form of this used as a first name; variant forms are **Lawrie, Lawry**.

Lawrence a variant form of **Laurence**; diminutive forms are **Larry, Lawrie, Lawry**.

Lawrie, Lawry diminutive forms of **Lawrence**; a variant form of **Laurie**.

Lawson a surname, meaning son of Lawrence, used as a first name (*Old English*).

Lawton a surname, meaning from the place on the hill, now used as a first name (*Old English*).

Layton a variant form of **Leighton**.

Lazarus destitute of help (*Hebrew*).

Leander lion man (*Greek*).

Lee a surname, meaning field or meadow, used as a first name (*Old English*); a variant form is **Leigh**.

Leif beloved one (*Old Norse*).

Leigh a variant form of **Lee**.

Leighton a surname, meaning

herb garden, used as a first name (*Old English*); a variant form is **Layton**.

Leland a variant form of **Leyland**.

Lemuel devoted to God (*Hebrew*); a diminutive form is **Lem**.

Len a diminutive form of **Leonard, Lennox, Lionel**.

Lennard a variant form of **Leonard**.

Lennie a diminutive form of **Leonard, Lennox, Lionel**.

Lennox a placename and surname, meaning abounding in elm trees, used as a first name (*Scots Gaelic*).

Lenny a diminutive form of **Leonard, Lennox, Lionel**; a variant form is **Lonnie**.

Leo lion (*Latin*); a variant form is **Leon**.

Leon a variant form of **Leo**.

Leonard lion strong (*Germanic*); a variant form is **Lennard**; diminutive forms are **Len, Lennie, Lenny**.

Leonidas of a lion (*Greek*).

Leontius of the lion (*Latin*).

Leopold bold for the people (*Germanic*).

Leroy the king (*Old French*); a variant form is **Elroy**; diminutive forms are **Lee, Roy**.

Leslie a surname, meaning garden by water, used as a first name (*Gaelic*).

Lester a surname, meaning from the Roman site (i.e. the present city of Leicester), used as a first name (*Old English*).

Levi joined (*Hebrew*).

Lewis bold warrior (*Germanic*); diminutive forms are **Lew, Lewie**.

Lex a diminutive form of **Alexander**.

Leyland a surname, meaning fallow or untilled land, used as a first name (*Old English*); a variant form is **Leland**.

Liam the Irish form of **William**.

Lincoln a placename and surname, meaning the place by the pool, used as a first name (*Celtic/Latin*).

Lindall, Lindell a surname, meaning valley of lime trees, used as a first name (*Old English*).

Lindley a placename and surname, meaning lime tree meadow or flax field, used as a first name (*Old English*); a variant form is **Linley**.

Lindsay, Lindsey a surname, meaning island of Lincoln, used as a first name; variant forms are **Linsay, Linsey, Linzi, Lynsay, Lynsey**.

Linford a surname, meaning from the ford of the lime tree or flax field, used as a first name (*Old English*).

Linley a variant form of **Lindley**.

Linsay, Linsey variant forms of **Lindsay**.

Linton a surname, meaning flax place, used as a first name (*Old English*).

Linus flaxen-haired (*Greek*).

Lionel young lion (*Latin*); a diminutive form is **Len**.

Lisle a surname, meaning island, or from Lisle in Normandy, used as a first name (*Old French*); variant forms are **Lyall, Lyle**.

Litton a placename and surname, meaning loud torrent, used as a first name (*Old English*); a variant form is **Lytton**.

Llewelyn lion-like (*Welsh*).

Lloyd a surname, meaning grey, used as a first name (*Welsh*).

Locke a surname, meaning enclosure, stronghold, used as a first name (*Old English*).

Logan a surname, meaning little hollow, used as a first name (*Scots Gaelic*).

Lombard a surname, meaning long beard, used as a first name (*Germanic*).

Lonnie a variant form of **Lenny**.

Lorcan, Lorcán fierce (*Irish Gaelic*).

Loring a surname, meaning man from Lorraine (bold and famous), used as a first name (*Germanic/Old French*).

Lorn a variant form of **Lorne**.

Lorne a Scottish placename (the northern area of Argyll), of uncertain meaning, used as a first name; a variant form is **Lorn**.

Lot a veil; a covering (*Hebrew*).

Lou a diminutive form of **Louis**.

Louis the French form of **Lewis**; diminutive forms are **Lou, Louie**.

Lovel, Lovell a surname, meaning little wolf, used as a first name (*Old French*); a variant form is **Lowell**.

Lowell a variant form of **Lovel**.

Luc the French form of **Luke**.

Luca the Italian form of **Luke**.

Lucan a placename, meaning place of elms, used as a first name (*Irish Gaelic*).

Lucas a variant form of **Luke**.

Lucian belonging to or sprung from Lucius (*Latin*).

Lucien a French form of **Lucian**.

Lucifer light bringer (*Latin*).

Lucius from *lux*, light (*Latin*).

Ludovic, Ludovick variant forms of of **Lewis**; a diminutive form is **Ludo**.

Ludwig the German form of **Lewis**.

Luis a Spanish form of **Lewis**.

Luke light (*Latin*).

Luther illustrious warrior (*Germanic*).

Lyall a variant form of **Lisle**.

Lycurgus wolf driver (*Greek*).

Lyle a variant form of **Lisle**.

Lynden, Lyndon a surname, meaning dweller by lime trees, used as a first name; a diminutive form is **Lyn**.

Lynn a surname, meaning pool or waterfall, used as a first name (*Celtic*); diminutive forms are **Lyn, Lin, Linn**; also used as a girl's name.

Lynsay, Lynsey variant forms of **Lindsay**.

Lysander liberator (*Greek*); a diminutive form is **Sandy**.

Lyss a diminutive form of **Ulysses**.

Lytton a variant form of **Litton**.

Madison a surname, meaning son of Matthew or Maud, used as a first name (*Old English*).

Madoc good; beneficent (*Welsh*).

Magee a surname, meaning son of Hugh, used a first name (*Irish Gaelic*).

Magnus great (*Latin*).

Maitland a surname, meaning unproductive land, used as a first name (*Old French*).

Malachi messenger of Jehovah (*Hebrew*).

Malcolm servant of Columba (*Scots Gaelic*); diminutive forms are **Calum, Mal**.

Malise servant of Jesus (*Scots Gaelic*).

Mallory a surname, meaning unfortunate, luckless, used as a first name (*Old French*).

Malone a surname, meaning

follower of St John, sometimes used as a first name (*Irish Gaelic*).

Manasseh one who causes to forget (*Hebrew*).

Manfred man of peace (*Germanic*); a diminutive form is **Manny**.

Manley a surname, meaning brave, upright, used as a first name (*Middle English*).

Manny diminutive forms of **Emmnauel, Immanuel, Manfred**.

Manuel the Spanish form of **Emmanuel**.

Marc a French form of **Mark**; a variant form of **Marcus**.

Marcel a French form of **Marcellus**.

Marcus the Latin form of **Mark**, now used as an English variant form; a variant form is **Marc**.

Marius martial (*Latin*).

Mark a hammer; a male; sprung from Mars (*Latin*); a variant form is **Marcus**.

Marland a surname, meaning lake land, used as a first name (*Old English*).

Marlo a variant form of **Marlow, Marlowe**.

Marlon of uncertain meaning, possibly hawk-like (*French*).

Marlow, Marlowe a placename and surname, meaning land of the former pool, used as a first name (*Old English*); a variant forms is **Marlo**.

Marmaduke a mighty noble; Madoc's servant (*Celtic*); a diminutive form is **Duke**.

Marshall a surname, meaning horse servant, used as a first name (*Germanic*).

Marston a surname, meaning place by a marsh, used as a first name (*Old English*).

Martin of Mars; warlike (*Latin*); a variant form is **Martyn**; a diminutive form is **Marty**.

Marty a diminutive form of **Martin**.

Martyn a variant form of **Martin**.

Marvin a variant form of **Mervin**.

Mat a diminutive form of **Matthew**.

Matheson, Mathieson a surname, meaning son of Matthew, now used as a first name.

Mathias a variant form of **Matthias**.

Matt a diminutive form of **Matthew**.

Matthew gift of Jehovah

(*Hebrew*); diminutive forms are
Mat, Matt, Mattie.

Matthias a Latin form of
Matthew; a variant form is
Mathias.

Mattie a diminutive form of
Matthew.

Maurice Moorish, dark-coloured
(*Latin*); a diminutive form is
Mo.

Maurus from Mauritania,
Moorish (*Latin*).

Max a diminutive form of
Maximilian, Maxwell, also
used independently; a diminutive form is **Maxie**.

Maxie a diminutive form of
Max, Maximilian, Maxwell.

Maximilian the greatest, a
combination of *Maximus* and
Aemilianus (*Latin*); diminutive
forms are **Max, Maxie**.

Maximilien the French form of
Maximilian.

Maxwell a surname, meaning
spring of Magnus, used as a
first name; a diminutive form is
Max.

Maynard a surname, meaning
strong, brave, used as a first
name (*Germanic*).

Medwin a surname, meaning
mead friend, used as a first
name (*Old English*).

Mel a diminutive form of
Melville, Melvin, Melvyn.

Melbourne a surname, meaning
mill stream, used as a first
name (*Old English*).

Melchior of uncertain meaning,
possibly king of light; in the
Bible, one of the three kings
(*Hebrew*).

Melfyn from Carmarthen
(*Welsh*).

Melville, Melvin, Melvyn a
surname, meaning Amalo's
place, used as a first name (*Old
French*); a diminutive form is
Mel.

Mercer a surname, meaning
merchant, used as a first name
(*Old French*).

Meredith a surname, meaning
lord, used as a first name
(*Welsh*).

Merfyn eminent matter (*Welsh*).

Merle blackbird (*Old French*); a
variant form of **Meriel**.

Merlin, Merlyn sea fort (*Welsh*).

Merrill a surname, meaning son
of Muriel (*Celtic*) or pleasant
place (*Old English*), used as a
first name; variant forms are
Meryl, Merryll.

Merryll a variant form of
Merrill.

Merton a surname, meaning

farmstead by the pool, used as a first name (*Old English*).

Mervin, Mervyn a surname, meaning famous friend, used as a first name (*Old English*); a variant form is **Marvin**; anglicized forms of **Merfyn**.

Meyer a variant form of **Mayer**.

Micah who is like unto Jehovah? (*Hebrew*).

Michael who is like unto God? (*Hebrew*); diminutive forms are **Mick, Micky, Mike**.

Michel the French form of **Michael**; a German diminutive of **Michael**.

Mick, Micky diminutive forms of **Michael**.

Mike a diminutive form of **Michael**.

Miles a soldier (*Germanic*); a variant form is **Myles**.

Milford a placename and surname, meaning mill ford, used as a first name (*Old English*).

Miller a surname, meaning miller, grinder, used as a first name (*Old English*); a variant form is **Milner**.

Millward a variant form of **Milward**.

Milne a surname, meaning at the mill, used as a first name (*Old English*).

Milner a variant form of **Miller**.

Milo the Greek samson (*Greek*).

Milton a surname, meaning middle farmstead or mill farm, used as a first name (*Old English*); a diminutive form is **Milt**.

Milward a surname, meaning mill keeper, used as a first name (*Old English*); a variant form is **Millward**.

Mitchell a surname form of **Michael**.

Mo diminutive form of **Maurice, Morris**.

Modred counsellor; in Arthurian legend the knight who killed King Arthur (*Old English*).

Monroe, Monro a surname, meaning mouth of the Roe river, used as a first name (*Irish Gaelic*); variant forms are **Munro, Munroe, Munrow**.

Montague, Montagu a surname, meaning pointed hill, used as a first name; a diminutive form is **Monty**.

Montgomery, Montgomerie a surname, meaning hill of the powerful man, sometimes used as a first name (*Old French/Germanic*); a diminutive form is **Monty**.

Monty a diminutive form of **Montague, Montgomery**.

Moray a variant form of **Murray**.

Morgan sea-dweller (*Celtic*).

Morley a surname, meaning moor meadow, used as a first name (*Old English*).

Morrice, Morris variant forms of **Maurice**; a diminutive form is **Mo**.

Mortimer a surname, meaning dead sea, used as a first name (*Old French*).

Morton a surname, meaning farmstead moor, used as a first name (*Old English*).

Moses meaning uncertain, most probably an Egyptian name (*Hebrew*).

Muir a form of the surname Moore, meaning moor (*Old French*), used as a first name.

Mungo amiable (*Gaelic*).

Munro, Munroe, Munrow variant forms of **Monroe**.

Murdo, Murdoch sea-warrior (*Scots Gaelic*).

Murray a surname, meaning seaboard place used as a first name; a variant form is **Moray**.

Myles a variant form of **Miles**; devotee of Mary (*Irish Gaelic*).

Myron fragrant oil (*Greek*).

Nairn dweller by the alder tree (*Celtic*).

Nathan gift (*Hebrew*); a diminutive form is **Nat**.

Nathaniel, Nathanael God gave (*Hebrew*); a diminutive form is **Nat**.

Neal, Neale variant forms of **Neil**.

Ned, Neddie, Neddy (a contraction of 'mine Ed') diminutive forms of **Edgar, Edmund, Edward, Edwin**.

Neil champion (*Gaelic*); variant forms are **Neal, Neale, Nial, Niall**.

Nelson a surname, meaning son of Neil, used as a first name.

Nestor coming home (*Greek*).

Neven a variant form of **Nevin**.

Neville a placename and surname, meaning new place,

used as a first name (*Old French*).

Nevin a surname, meaning little saint, used as a first name (*Irish Gaelic*); variant forms are **Nevin, Niven**.

Newman a surname, meaning newcomer, new settler, used as a first name (*Old English*).

Newton a surname, meaning new farmstead or village, used as a first name (*Old English*).

Nial, Niall variant forms of **Neil**.

Nicholas victory of the people (*Greek*); a variant form is **Nicolas**; diminutive forms are **Nick, Nicky**.

Nick a diminutive form of **Nicholas, Nicol**.

Nicky a diminutive form of **Nicholas, Nicol**.

Nicol a Scottish surname form of **Nicholas** used as a first name.

Nigel black (*Latin*).

Ninian meaning uncertain; the name of a 5th-century saint (*Celtic*).

Noah rest (*Hebrew*).

Noël, Noel Christmas (*French*).

Nolan a surname, meaning son of the champion, used as a first name (*Irish Gaelic*).

Noll, Nollie diminutive forms of **Oliver**.

Norman northman (*Germanic*); a diminutive form is **Norrie**.

Norton a surname, meaning northern farmstead or village, used as a surname (*Old English*).

Norville a surname, meaning north town, used as a first name (*Old French*).

Norvin northern friend (*Old English*).

Nowell an English form of **Noël**.

Nye a diminutive form of **Aneurin**.

Obed serving God (*Hebrew*).
Oberon a variant form of **Auberon**.

Octavius eighth (*Latin*).
Ogden oak valley (*Old English*).
Ogilvie a surname, meaning high

peak, used as a first name (*Celtic*).

Oliver an olive tree (*Latin*); diminutive forms are **Ollie, Olly, Noll, Nollie**.

Ollie, Olly diminutive forms of **Oliver**.

Omar first son (*Arabic*).

Oran pale-skinned man (*Gaelic*); variant forms are **Orin, Orrin**.

Oren laurel (*Hebrew*).

Orin a variant form of **Oran**.

Orion son of light (*Greek*).

Orlando the Italian form of **Roland**.

Orson little bear (*Latin*).

Orville, Orvil golden place (*Old French*).

Osbert god-bright (*Old English*); a diminutive form is **Ossie**.

Osborn, Osborne, Osbourne a surname, meaning divine bear, or warrior, used a first name (*Germanic*) a diminutive form is **Ossie**.

Oscar divine spear (*Germanic*); a diminutive form is **Ossie**.

Osmond, Osmund divine protection (*Germanic*); a diminutive form is **Ossie**.

Ossie a diminutive form of **Osbert, Osborn, Oscar, Osmond, Oswald**.

Oswald divine rule (*Germanic*).

Otis a surname, meaning son of Ote, used as a first name (*Germanic*).

Owain a Welsh form of **Eugene**.

Owen a lamb; a young warrior (*Celtic*).

Oz, Ozzie, Ozzy diminutive forms of names beginning with *Os-*.

Paddy a diminutive form of **Patrick**.

Padraig the Irish Gaelic form of **Patrick**.

Pat a diminutive form of **Patrick**.

Patrick noble; a patrician (*Latin*); a variant form is **Patric,** diminutive forms are **Paddy, Pat**.

Paul little (*Latin*).

Percival, Perceval pierce valley (*Old French*).

Percy a surname, meaning from Perci-en-Auge in Normandy, used as a first name (*Old French*).

Peregrine wanderer (*Latin*); a diminutive form is **Perry**.

Perry diminutive form of **Peregrine**, now used in its own right; a surname, meaning pear tree, used as a first name (*Old English*).

Peter stone (*Latin*); the diminutive form is **Pete**.

Phelim always good (*Irish*).

Phil a diminutive form of **Philip**, **Phillip**.

Philbert very bright (*Germanic*).

Philip lover of horses (*Greek*); a variant form is **Phillip**; diminutive forms are **Phil**, **Pip**.

Phillip a variant form of **Philip**; diminutive forms are **Phil**, **Pip**.

Phineas, Phinehas serpent's mouth (*Hebrew*).

Pierce a surname form of **Piers**, used as a first name.

Pierre the French form of **Peter**.

Piers a variant form of **Peter**.

Pierse a surname form of **Piers**, used as a first name.

Pip a diminutive form of **Philip**, **Phillip**.

Presley a surname, meaning dweller in the priests' meadow, used as a first name (*Old English*).

Primo first born (*Latin*).

Pugh a surname, meaning son of Hugh, used as a first name (*Welsh*).

Quentin fifth (*Latin*); a variant form is **Quinton**.

Quincy, Quincey a surname, meaning fifth place, used as a first name (*Latin/French*).

Quinlan well formed (*Irish Gaelic*).

Quinn a surname, meaning wise, used as a first name (*Irish Gaelic*).

Quinton a variant form of **Quentin**.

Quintus fifth (*Latin*).

Rab, Rabbie diminutive forms of **Robert**.

Radcliffe a surname, meaning red cliff, used as a first name (*Old English*).

Radley a surname, meaning red meadow, used as a first name (*Old English*).

Rafe a variant form of **Ralph**.

Ralph famous wolf or hero (*Germanic*); variant forms are **Rafe, Rolph**.

Ram height (*Hebrew*).

Ramsay, Ramsey a placename and surname, meaning wild garlic, river island, used as a first name (*Old Norse*).

Ramsden Ram's valley (*Old English*).

Ranald a variant form of **Reginald**.

Rand a diminutive form of **Randal, Randolf**.

Randal, Randall a surname diminutive form of **Randolph** used as a first name (*Old English*); a variant form is **Ranulf**.

Randolf, Randolph shield-wolf (*Germanic*); a variant form is **Ranulf**; diminutive forms are **Rand, Randy**.

Randy a diminutive form of **Randolf**, also used independently.

Rankin, Rankine a diminutive surname form of **Randolph** used as a first name.

Ransom a surname, meaning son of Rand, used as a first name.

Ranulf a variant form of **Randolf**.

Raoul the French form of **Ralph**.

Raphael the healing of God (*Hebrew*).

Ras a diminutive form of **Erasmus, Erastus**.

Rasmus a diminutive form of **Erasmus**.

Rastus a diminutive form of **Erastus**.

Rawnsley a surname, meaning Raven's meadow, used as a first name (*Old English*).

Ray a diminutive form of

Raymond, now used independently; a variant form is **Rae**.

Raymond, Raymund wise protection (*Germanic*); a diminutive form is **Ray**.

Rayne a surname, meaning mighty army (*Germanic*), used as a first name; a variant form is **Rayner**.

Rayner a variant form of **Rayne**.

Read, Reade a surname, meaning red headed, used as a first name (*Old English*); variant forms are **Reed, Reede**.

Reagan a variant form of **Regan**.

Reardon a variant form of **Riordan**.

Redding a variant form of **Reading**.

Redmond counsel profection (*Germanic*); a variant form is **Redman**.

Reece a surname form of **Rhys** used as a first name.

Reed, Reede variant forms of **Read**.

Rees the English form of **Rhys**.

Reeve, Reeves steward, bailiff (*Old English*).

Regan a surname, meaning little king, used as a first name (*Irish Gaelic*); variant forms are **Reagan, Rogan**.

Reginald counsel rule (*Germanic*); diminutive forms are **Reg, Reggie**.

Reilly a surname, meaning valiant, used as a first name (*Irish Gaelic*); a variant form is **Riley**.

Reinald an early English form of **Reginald**.

Remus power (*Latin*).

René born again (*French*).

Rennie, Renny a diminutive surname form of Reynold used as a first name.

Reuben behold a son (*Hebrew*); a diminutive form is **Rube**.

Rex king (*Latin*).

Reynard brave advice (*Germanic*); fox (*French*).

Reynold strong rule (*Germanic*).

Rhodri circle ruler (*Welsh*).

Rhys ardour (*Welsh*).

Rich a diminutive form of **Richard, Richman, Richmond**.

Richard a strong king; powerful (*Germanic*); diminutive forms are **Dick, Rich, Richey, Richie, Rick, Rickie, Ricky, Ritchie**.

Richey, Richie diminutive forms of **Richard, Richman, Richmond**.

Richman a variant form of **Richmond**.

Richmond a surname, meaning strong hill, used as a first name (*Old French*); a variant form is **Richman**; diminutive forms are **Rich, Richey, Richie**.

Ridley a surname, meaning cleared meadow, used as a first name (*Old English*).

Riley a variant form of **Reilly**.

Riordan a surname, meaning bard, used as a first name (*Irish Gaelic*); a variant form is **Reardon**.

Ritchie a diminutive and surname form of **Richard**.

Roald famous ruler (*Old Norse*).

Robert bright in fame (*Germanic*); diminutive forms are **Bob, Bobby, Rab, Rob, Robbie, Robby, Robin**.

Robin a diminutive form of **Robert**, now used independently; a variant form is **Robyn**.

Robinson a surname, meaning son of Robert, used as a first name (*Old English*).

Robyn a variant form of **Robin**.

Rock stone or oak (*Old English*).

Rod a diminutive form of **Roderick, Rodney**.

Roddy a diminutive form of **Roderick, Rodney**.

Roderic, Roderick fame power-ful (*Germanic*); diminutive forms are **Rod, Roddy, Rurik**.

Rodger a variant form of **Roger**.

Rodney from a reed island (*Old English*): diminutive forms are **Rod,** Roddy.

Rogan a variant form of **Regan**.

Roger famous with the spear (*Germanic*); a variant form is **Rodger**.

Rohan healing, incense (*Sanskrit*).

Roland, Rolland fame of the land (*Germanic*); variant forms are **Rolland, Rowland**; a diminutive form is **Roly**.

Rolf a contraction of **Rudolf**; a variant form is **Rollo**.

Rollo a variant form of **Rolf**.

Rolph a variant form of **Ralph**.

Roly a diminutive form of **Roland**.

Romilly a surname, meaning broad clearing (*Old English*) or place of Romilius (*Old French*), used as a first name.

Ron a diminutive form of **Ronald**.

Ronald a variant form of **Reginald**; diminutive forms are **Ron, Ronnie, Ronny**.

Ronan little seal (*Irish Gaelic*).

Ronnie, Ronny diminutive forms of **Ronald**.

Rooney red, red-complexioned (*Gaelic*).

Rory red (*Irish and Scots Gaelic*).

Roscoe a surname, meaning deer wood, used as a first name (*Old Norse*).

Roslin, Roslyn a placename, meaning unploughable land by the pool, used as first name (*Scots Gaelic*); a variant form is **Rosslyn**.

Ross a placename and surname, meaning promontory, used as a first name (*Scots Gaelic*).

Rosslyn a variant form of **Roslin**.

Rowan red (*Irish Gaelic*).

Rowe a surname, meaning hedgerow, used as a first name (*Old English*).

Rowell a surname, meaning rough hill, used as a first name (*Old English*).

Rowland a variant form of **Roland**.

Rowley a surname, meaning rough meadow, used as a first name (*Old English*).

Roy red (*Gaelic*); king (*Old French*).

Royal a variant form of **Royle**.

Royce a surname form of **Rose** used as a first name.

Royston a surname, meaning place of Royce, now used as a first name (*Germanic/Old English*).

Rube a diminutive form of **Reuben**.

Rudi a diminutive form of **Rudolf**.

Rudolf, Rudolph famous wolf; hero (*Germanic*).

Rudyard reed enclosure (*Old English*).

Rufe a diminutive form of Rufus.

Rufus red-haired (*Latin*); a diminutive form is **Rufe**.

Rupert an anglicized Germanic form of **Robert**.

Rurik a diminutive form of **Roderick, Roderic**.

Russell a surname meaning, red hair, used as a first name (*Old French*); a diminutive form is **Russ**.

Rutherford a surname, meaning cattle ford, used as a first name (*Old English*).

Ryan the Irish surname of uncertain meaning used as a first name.

Rye From the riverbank (*French*).

Rylan, Ryland a surname, meaning where rye grows, used as a first name (*Old English*).

Sam a diminutive form of **Samuel**, now used independently.

Sammy a diminutive form of **Samuel**.

Samson, Sampson like the sun (*Hebrew*).

Samuel name of God, or heard by God (*Hebrew*); diminutive forms are **Sam, Sammy**.

Sanders from Alexander (*Old English*); a diminutive form is **Sandy**.

Sandy a diminutive form of **Alexander, Lysander, Sanders**.

Sanford a surname, meaning sandy ford, used as a first name (*Old English*).

Saul asked for by God (*Hebrew*).

Scott a surname, meaning of Scotland, used as a first name.

Sealey a variant form of **Seeley**.

Seamas, Seamus Irish Gaelic forms of **James**.

Sean an Irish Gaelic form of **John**.

Searle a surname, meaning armed warrior, used as a first name (*Germanic*).

Seaton a placename and surname, meaning farmstead at the sea, used as a first name (*Old English*); a variant form is **Seton**.

Sebastian august, majestic (*Greek*).

Secundus second born (*Latin*).

Seeley a first name, meaning blessed and happy, used as a first name (*Old English*); a variant form is **Sealey**.

Selby a placename and surname, meaning place by the willow trees, used as a first name (*Old English*).

Selden From the valley of the willow tree (*Old English*).

Selig blessed, happy one (*Yiddish*); a variant form is **Zelig**.

Selwyn, Selwin wild (*Germanic*).

Septimus seventh (*Latin*).

Seth appointed (*Hebrew*).

Seton a variant form of **Seaton**.

Seumas a Gaelic form of **James**.

Sexton a surname, meaning sacristan, used as a first name (*Old French*).

Sextus sixth (*Latin*).

Seymour a surname, meaning from Saint-Maur in France, used as a first name (*Old French*).

Shamus an anglicized form of **Seamus**.

— **Shane** an anglicized form of **Sean**.

Shaw a surname, meaning small wood or grove, used as a first name (*Old English*).

Shawn, Shaun anglicized forms of **Sean**.

Sheldon a surname, meaning heathery hill with a shed, flat-topped hill, or steep valley, used as a first name (*Old English*).

Shepard a surname, meaning sheep herder, shepherd, used as a first name (*Old English*).

Sheridan a surname, meaning seeking, used as a first name (*Irish Gaelic*).

Sherlock fair-haired (*Old English*).

Sherman a surname, meaning shearman, used as a first name (*Old English*).

Sherwood a placename and surname, meaning shore wood, used as a first name (*Old English*).

Siddall, Siddell a surname, meaning broad slope, used as a first name (*Old English*).

Sidney one who lives on a wide island (*Old English*); a variant form is **Sydney**; a diminutive form is **Sid**.

Siegfried victory peace (*Germanic*).

Silas a shortened form of **Silvanus**.

Silvester of a wood (*Latin*); a variant form is **Sylvester**; a diminutive form is **Sly**.

Sim a diminutive form of **Simon, Simeon**.

Simon, Simeon hearing with acceptance (*Hebrew*); diminutive forms are **Sim, Simmy**.

Sinclair a surname, meaning from St Clair in France, used as a first name (*Old French*); a variant form is **St Clair**.

Sly a diminutive form of **Silvester, Sylvester**.

Sol the sun (*Latin*); a diminutive form of **Solomon**.

Solly a diminutive form of **Solomon**.

Solomon peaceable (*Hebrew*); diminutive forms are **Sol, Solly**.

Somerled summer traveller (*Old Norse*).

Somerton a placename, meaning summer farmstead, used as a first name (*Old English*).

Somhairle an Irish and Scots Gaelic form of **Somerled**.

Sorley an anglicized form of **Somhairle**.

Sorrel sour (*Germanic*), the name of a salad plant used as a first name.

Spencer a surname, meaning steward or dispenser, used as a first name (*Old French*).

St John Saint John (pronounced *sinjon*).

Stacey a diminutive form of **Eustace**, used independently.

Stafford a surname, meaning ford by a landing place, used as a first name (*Old English*).

Stamford a variant form of **Stanford**.

Standish a surname, meaning stony pasture, used as a first name (*Old English*).

Stanford a surname, meaning stone ford, used as a first name (*Old English*); a variant form is **Stamford**.

Stanhope a surname, meaning stony hollow, used as a first name (*Old English*).

Stanley a surname and placename meaning stony field, used as a first name (*Old English*).

Stanton a surname, meaning stony farmstead, used as first name (*Old English*).

Stefan a German form of **Stephen**.

Stephen, Steven crown (*Greek*); diminutive forms are **Steve, Stevie**.

Sterling a surname, meaning little star, used as a first name (*Old English*); a variant form is **Stirling**.

Stewart a variant and surname form of **Stuart**.

Stirling a variant form of **Sterling**; a placename, meaning enclosed land by the stream, used as a first name (*Scottish Gaelic*).

Stoddard a surname, meaning horse keeper, used as a first name (*Old English*).

Stowe a surname, meaning holy place, used as a first name (*Old English*).

Strachan, Strahan a surname, meaning little valley, used as a first name (*Scots Gaelic*).

Stratford a placename, meaning ford on a Roman road, used as a first name (*Old English*).

Stuart, Stewart, Steuart the surname meaning steward used as a first name (*Old English*).

Sullivan a surname, meaning black-eyed, used as a first name (*Irish Gaelic*).

Sumner a surname, meaning one who summons, used as a first name (*Old French*).

Sutherland a placename and surname, meaning southern

land, used as a first name (*Old Norse*).

Sutton a placename and surname, meaning southern farmstead, used as a first name (*Old English*).

Sydney a variant form of **Sidney**.

Sylvester a variant form of **Silvester**; a diminutive form is **Sly**.

Tad a diminutive form of **Thaddeus**, also used independently.

Tadhg an Irish Gaelic form of **Thaddeus**; a variant form is **Teague**.

Taffy Welsh form of David (*Celtic*).

Talbot a surname, meaning command of the valley, used as a first name (*Germanic*).

Tam (*Scots*) a diminutive form of **Thomas**.

Tancred thought strong (*Germanic*).

Tate a surname, meaning

cheerful, used as a first name (*Old Norse*); a variant form is **Tait**.

Tait a variant form of **Tate**.

Taylor a surname, meaning tailor, used as a first name (*Old French*).

Teague a variant form of **Tadhg**.

Ted, Teddie, Teddy diminutive forms of **Edward, Theodore, Theodoric**.

Tennison, Tennyson variant forms of **Dennison**.

Terence from a Roman family name of unknown origin (*Latin*); variant forms are

Terrance, Terrence; diminutive forms are **Tel, Terry**.

Terris, Terriss a surname, meaning son of Terence, used as a first name.

Tertius third (*Latin*).

Thaddeus gift of God (*Greek-Aramaic*); diminutive forms are **Tad, Thad, Thaddy**.

Thaine a surname, meaning holder of land in return for military service, used as a first name (*Old English*); a variant form is **Thane**.

Theo diminutive forms of **Theobald, Theodore, Theodora**.

Theobald bold for the people (*Germanic*); a diminutive form is **Theo**.

Theodore the gift of God (*Greek*); diminutive forms are **Ted, Teddie, Teddy, Theo**.

Theodoric, Theodorick people powerful (*Germanic*); diminutive forms are **Derek, Derrick, Dirk, Ted, Teddie, Teddy**.

Theodosius form of **Theodosia**.

Theophilus lover of God (*Greek*).

Thomas twin (*Aramaic*); diminutive forms are **Tam, Thom, Tom, Tommy**.

Thor thunder (*Old Norse*), in Norse mythology, the god of thunder; a variant form is **Tor**.

Thorburn a surname, meaning Thor's warrior or bear, used as a first name (*Old Norse*).

Thorp, Thorpe a surname, meaning farm village, used as a first name (*Old English*).

Thurstan, Thurston a surname, meaning Thor stone, used as a first name (*Old Norse*).

Tiernan, Tierney a surname, meaning lord, used as a first name (*Irish Gaelic*); a variant form is **Kiernan**.

Tim a diminutive form of **Timon, Timothy**.

Timon reward (*Greek*).

Timothy honouring God (*Greek*); diminutive forms are **Tim, Timmie, Timmy**.

Titus protected (*Latin*).

Tobias, Tobiah Jehovah is good (*Hebrew*); a diminutive form is **Toby**.

Toby a diminutive form of **Tobias**, now used independently.

Todd fox (*Latin*).

Tom a diminutive form of **Thomas**, now used independently.

Tommie, Tommy diminutive forms of **Thomas**.

Tony a diminutive form of **Antony**.

Tor a variant form of **Thor**.

Torquil God's cauldron (*Old Norse*).

Torr a surname, meaning tower (*Old English*) or bull (*Old French*) used as a first name.

Townsend, Townshend a surname, meaning end of the village, used as a first name (*Old English*).

Tracey a variant form of **Tracy**.

Tracy a surname, meaning Thracian, used as a first name (*Old French*); a variant form is **Tracey**.

Traherne a surname, meaning iron strength, used as a first name (*Welsh*).

Travers a surname, meaning crossing, crossroads, used as a first name (*Old French*); a variant form is **Travis**.

Travis a variant form of **Travers**.

Tremaine, Tremayne a surname, meaning homestead on the rock, used as a first name (*Cornish*).

Trent a river name, meaning liable to flood, used as a first name (*Celtic*).

Trev a diminutive form of **Trevor**.

Trevelyan a surname, meaning mill farm, used as a first name (*Cornish*).

Trevor a surname, meaning big river, used as a first name (*Welsh*); a diminutive form is **Trev**.

Tristram, Tristam grave; pensive (*Celtic*).

Tristan tumult (*Celtic*).

Troy a surname, meaning of Troyes, used as a first name (*Old French*); the name of the city in Asia Minor besieged by the Greeks, used as a first name.

True the adjective for the quality of being faithful and loyal used as a first name.

Trueman, Truman a surname, meaning faithful servant, used as a first name (*Old English*).

Trystan a Welsh form of **Tristan**.

Tudor a Welsh form of **Theodore**.

Turner a surname, meaning worker on a lathe, used as a first name (*Old French*).

Ty a diminutive form of **Tybalt, Tyler, Tyrone, Tyson**.

Tybalt a variant form of **Theobald**; a diminutive form is **Ty**.

Tye a surname, meaning enclosure, used as a first name (*Old English*).

Tyler a surname, meaning tile-maker, used as a first name (*Old English*); a diminutive form is **Ty**.

Tyrone a placename and surname, meaning land of Owen, used as a first name (*Irish Gaelic*); a diminutive form is **Ty**.

Tyson a surname, meaning fire-brand, used as a first name (*Old French*); a diminutive form is **Ty**.

Ulmar, Ulmer wolf (*Old English*).

Ulric, Ulrick wolf power (*Old English*); the English form of **Ulrich**.

Ulrich fortune and power (*Germanic*).

Ulysses angry, wrathful (*Greek*); a diminutive form is **Lyss**.

Unwin a surname, meaning not a friend, used as a first name (*Old English*).

Uri light (*Hebrew*).

Uriah fire of the Lord (*Hebrew*).

Urian a husbandman (*Danish*).

Uriel light of God (*Hebrew*).

Vachel little calf (*Old French*).

Val a diminutive form of **Valentine**.

Valentine strong, healthy, powerful (*Latin*); a diminutive form is **Val**.

Valerian strong, powerful (*Latin*).

Van a prefix in Dutch surnames, now used independently as an English-language first name.

Vance young (*Old English*).

Vaughan, Vaughn a surname, meaning small one, used as a first name (*Welsh*).

Vere a surname, meaning from Ver in France, used as a first name (*Old French*).

Vernon a surname, meaning alder tree, used as a first name (*Old French*).

Victor conqueror (*Latin*); a diminutive form is **Vic**.

Vincent conquering; victorious (*Latin*); diminutive forms are **Vin, Vince, Vinnie, Vinny**.

Vinnie, Vinny diminutive forms of **Vincent**.

Virgil, Vergil staff bearer (*Latin*), the name of the Roman poet of the 1st century BC;.

Vitus life (*Latin*).

Vivian, Vyvian full of life (*Latin*);

Wade a surname, meaning to go, or at the ford, used as a first name (*Old English*).

Wainwright a surname, meaning maker of carts, used as a first name (*Old English*).

Walker a surname, meaning a fuller, used as a first name (*Old English*).

Wallace from Wales; a diminutive form is **Wally** (*Old English*).

Wallis a man who comes from Wales (*Old English*); a variant form is **Wallace**; a diminutive form is **Wally**.

Wally a diminutive form of **Wallace, Wallis**.

Walt a diminutive form of **Walter, Walton**.

Walter ruler of army, people (*Germanic*); diminutive forms are **Walt, Wat, Watty**.

Walton a surname, meaning farmstead of the Britons, sometimes used as a first name (*Old English*); a diminutive form is **Walt**.

Ward a surname, meaning watchman; guard, used as a first name (*Old English*).

Warren a surname, meaning wasteland or game park, used as a first name (*Old French*).

Warwick a placename and surname, meaning dwellings by the weir, used as a first name (*Old English*).

Wat, Watty a diminutive form of **Walter**.

Wayne a surname, meaning a carter, used as a first name.

Webster a surname, meaning woman weaver, used as a first name (*Old English*).

Wendel, Wendell of the Wend people (*Germanic*); a variant form is **Wendel**.

Wesley a surname, meaning west wood, made famous by the Methodists John and Charles Wesley, used as a first name (*Old English*); a diminutive form is **Wes**.

Whitaker a surname, meaning white acre, used as a first name (*Old English*); a variant form is **Whittaker**.

Whitman a surname, meaning white- or fair-haired, used as a first name (*Old English*).

Whitney a surname and placename, meaning white island or Witta's island, used as a first name (*Old English*).

Whittaker a variant form of **Whitaker**.

Wilbert well-born (*Old English*).

Wilbur wild boar (*Old English*).

Wilfrid, Wilfred will peace (*Germanic*); a diminutive form is **Wilf**.

Will, Willie, Willy diminutive forms of **William**.

Willard a surname, meaning bold resolve, used as a first name (*Old English*).

Willemot resolute in spirit (*Germanic*).

William resolute helmet (*Germanic*); diminutive forms are **Bill, Will**.

Wilmer famous will or desire (*Old English*).

Wilson, Willson a surname, meaning son of Will, used as a first name (*Old English*).

Windham a variant form of **Wyndham**.

Winston a placename and surname, meaning friend's place or farm, used as a first name (*Old English*).

Winton a surname, meaning friend's farm, used as a first name (*Old English*).

Woodrow a surname, meaning row (of houses) in a wood, sometimes used as a first name;

a diminutive form is **Woody**.

Woody a diminutive form of **Woodrow**, used independently.

Wyman a surname, meaning battle protector, used as a first name (*Old English*).

Wyn white (*Welsh*); a variant form is **Wynn**.

Wyndham a surname, meaning homestead of Wyman, used as a first name (*Old English*); a variant form is **Windham**.

Wynn, Wynne a surname, meaning friend, used as a first name; a variant form of **Wyn**.

Xavier a placename, meaning new house owner, used as a first name (*Spanish/Basque*).

Xenos stranger (*Greek*).

Xerxes royal (*Persian*).

Yale a surname, meaning fertile upland (*Welsh*).

Yehudi a Jew (*Hebrew*).

Yves yew tree (*French-Germanic*).

Zabdiel gift of God (*Hebrew*).

Zaccheus innocent; pure (*Hebrew*).

Zachary, Zachariah, Zacharias, Zecheriah Jehovah has remembered (*Hebrew*); diminutive forms are **Zach, Zack, Zak**.

Zadok righteous (*Hebrew*).

Zeb a diminutive form of **Zebadiah, Zebedee, Zebulun**.

Zebadiah, Zebedee gift of the Lord (*Hebrew*).

Zebulon, Zebulun elevation (*Hebrew*); diminutive forms are **Lonny, Zeb**.

Zedekiah justice of the Lord (*Hebrew*); a diminutive form is **Zed**.

Zeke a diminutive form of **Ezekiel**.

Zelig a variant form of **Selig**.

Zenas gift of Zeus (*Greek*).

Zephaniah hid of the Lord (*Hebrew*); a diminutive form is **Zeph**.